Adelma Grenier Simmons

The Pride of Cooks

Herbal Recipes from the Caprilands Kitchen

Photographed by George Gregory Wieser

MALLARD PRESS

MALLARD PRESS
An Imprint of BDD Promotional Book Company, Inc.
666 Fifth Avenue
New York, NY 10103

This book is meant to be educational in nature and is in no way meant to be used for self-treatment or self-diagnosis. Keep in mind that excess quantities of some herbs can be dangerous. The editors have attempted to include, wherever appropriate, cautions and guidelines for using the herbs and herbal recipes in the book. Yet, we realize that it is impossible for us to anticipate every conceivable use of herbs and every possible problem any use could cause. Moreover, we cannot know just what kinds of physical reactions or allergies some of you might have to substances discussed in this book.

For this reason, Mallard Press cannot assume responsibility for the effects of using the herbs or other information in this book. And we urge that all potentially serious health problems be managed by a physician.

Copyright © 1992 by Adelma Grenier Simmons
Photographs copyright © 1992 by
George Gregory Wieser

Produced by Wieser & Wieser, Inc.
118 East 25th Street,
New York, NY 10010

Editorial Development by Beverly Pennacchini
Design, Typography and Production by Tony Meisel
Photographic Styling by Laurie Pepin

Mallard Press and its accompanying design and logo are trademarks of the BDD Promotional Book Company, Inc.
First published in the United States of America
in 1992 by The Mallard Press.

ISBN 0-7924-5616-5

Contents

The Pride of Cooks

Through the centuries, man has explored and recorded his findings in the world of herbs. Herb lore was collected by men and woman in all walks of life—physicians, poets, monks and housewives handed down a world of herbal knowledge on what can cure us, what can promise a bountiful harvest, the return of an errant love, or a tasty soup or salad.

All of us who study, write, talk about, grow or cook with herbs owe a great debt to the past, for herbal history invests even the most humble stew with an aura of romantic legend. Every season in the garden brings a new set of recipes, old and new to our kitchen at Caprilands. Spring, summer, autumn and winter-all have added meaning, for to each season the garden yields a special taste and presents a picture uniquely its own.

5

Tender Spring

A New England Spring is always the intermingling of two seasons. Winter is reluctant to remove its icy hold completely, yet seems to have great moments of indecision, when spring peeps coyly in and disappears at a shake of old winter's whiskers.

It is an anxious time for those who garden. The melting glances of spring expose roots, and encourage a rush of green growth, which are delicious and long awaited as the first fresh taste of the young season, but also tender and vulnerable to sudden plunges in temperature.

There are chives, chive blossoms, Egyptian onion stalks, sweet cicely leaves and blossoms, parsley, violets and violet leaves. Sometimes, we are lucky enough to have camomile. Mint leaves at this time are green, or darkly purple, like the orange mint, adding a touch of vermilion to our spring picture.

Sorrel

Hardy perennial, 2 feet. Resembles the related and common dock of the fields. Leaves succulent, long and shield-shaped. Buy a plant, then allow it to multiply. It is difficult to obtain seeds. Prefers sun to partial shade in rich, well-drained soil. Use in sorrel soup, sparingly in salads, as a sauce for beef, or cooked with beet tops, spinach, or cabbage.

Sorrel Bouillon

(Herbs— green sorrel, garlic, thyme)

1 handful of sorrel
1 clove garlic
3 grated onions
1/8 pound butter or margarine
6 cups chicken stock
3 large tomatoes
1 cup tomato juice
1/8 teaspoon thyme

Brown onion, sorrel and garlic in butter. Add stock and cook for 1/2 hour. Add tomatoes, (mashed or diced) and tomato juice and thyme, heat thoroughly. Strain if you wish to have a clear soup.

Calendula
(Pot Marigold)

The flowers, varying shades of orange and yellow, open at dawn and close at dusk. Grow pot marigolds from seed in rich soil. Prefers partial sun and will survive light frost. Lovely as a garnish or to add a light, fresh flavor to biscuits and soups.

Marigold Biscuits

1 cup fresh calendula flowers
    (pot marigold, or 1/2 cup dried)
1/4 cup chopped parsley
1 recipe baking powder biscuit dough (See cheese
    and sage biscuits recipe).

Add the calendula flowers and parsley to the biscuit dough and bake as usual. Makes 2 dozen.

Fennel

Perennial sometimes grown as an annual, 4 to 5 feet. The stems are blue-green, smooth and glossy, flattened at the base; leaves, bright green and feathery. Yellow flowers are produced in umbels. Propagate by sowing seeds in the spring after the soil is warm in full sun in average garden soil. Tender leaves and stems in relishes, salads, and as a garnish. Use leaves for flavoring in fish sauces, soups, and stews. Use ripe seeds to flavor puddings, spiced beets, sauerkraut, spaghetti, soups, breads, cakes, candy, and beverages.

Fennel and Escarole Salad

1 head escarole, cut into small pieces
1 large bunch fennel, cut finely to make 4 cups
6 stalks celery, finely chopped
2 green peppers, sliced
12 artichokes
4 hard-cooked eggs, cut in quarters
1 cooked Italian sausage, sliced
6 slices Italian mozzarella cheese, cut into strips
1 cup onions, chopped

Toss the above ingredients together and dress with a French dressing.

Sumptuous Summer

When the drowsy heat of summer hangs over the hillside herb garden, there is little time to do more than keep up with all the cooking, weeding, harvesting and story telling duties that present themselves in the height of the season.

The garden is bursting with sweetness. There is peppermint, apple and rose geraniums, rosemarys, thymes, lavenders, and a tall lemon geranium, to add zest and depth to our midsummer menu.

Caraway

Caraway is a hardy biennial, 1 to 3 feet in height with furrowed stems and finely cut leaves resembling the carrot's. Umbels of white flowers appear in June of the second year. Caraway prefers full sun and average, well-drained garden soil. Sow seeds in September for an early spring crop of leaves and seeds the following summer.

Caraway oil is extracted from the leaves and seeds. Young leaves are sometimes used in soup; seeds, in applesauce, apple pie, cookies, cakes and breads. The oil is used in perfume, soap and in making a liqueur called kummel. The thick, tapering roots, similar to parsnips but smaller, are considered a delicacy for the table. Harvest the brown crescent shaped seeds before they fall to the ground and before the birds begin to eat them, usually in August.

Rose Cookies

1 cup butter
1/2 cup honey
2 eggs, beaten
1 1/4 cups unbleached flour
1 1/2 cups whole wheat flour
1 teaspoon baking soda
1/2 teaspoon cream of tartar
2 tablespoons rose water or 1 teaspoon rose syrup
2 tablespoons caraway seeds
raisins for garnish

Preheat oven to 375. Cream together butter and honey. Add eggs and beat well. Sift flours with baking soda and cream of tartar. Add to creamed mixture. Stir in rose water or rose syrup and caraway seeds. Drop mixture by teaspoonfuls onto greased cookie sheets. Flatten slightly with moistened fingers and put a raisin in the center of each cookie. Bake in a 375 oven until lightly browned, about 8-10 minutes. Remove from cookie sheets and cool on a wire rack. Makes about 8 dozen

Thyme

Many varieties of thyme exist today. Some are dark green; others are more gray or yellow, some creep; others grow upward. Several have a distinctly citrus fragrance, but all have tiny oval leaves and many branches that grow close to the ground.

Thymus vulgaris is the common thyme used to season foods. Thyme is a perennial and may be grown from seed on one season. Creeping thymes grow best from plant divisions. All need sun and good drainage. Harvest thyme when dew has dried off. Thyme is used as a seasoning in poultry stuffing, seafood dishes, stews, and cajun recipes. It is often combined with rosemary, parsley and sage.

Summer Squash Soup

3 medium summer squash (yellow preferably)
4 cups chicken stock
1 cup chopped celery
3 medium onions, thinly sliced
1 clove garlic, crushed
1 sprig fresh rosemary, minced
1/2 cup chopped parsley

Wash, trim, and slice squash. Steam the squash until it is tender. Puree the cooked squash in a blender or a food processor and set it aside (about 1 1/2 cups puree). Bring the chicken stock to a boil in a large saucepan. Add celery, onions, garlic, rosemary and thyme and simmer, covered, about 10 minutes or until vegetables are tender. Reduce heat to low, add reserved squash puree and parsley. Cook to heat through. Yields 7 cups

Sweet Basil

Basil is a favorite kitchen herb that has a clove-like odor and flavor. Its bright green, toothed leaves are very fragrant, especially in the sun, but they wilt quickly. Its many varieties include small-leafed, bush, lemon, purple (also called dark opal), and cinnamon.

Basil is an annual that grows easily from seed and likes the hottest weather. Sow seeds three times during the year for a constant fresh crop during the summer months. It likes a rich soil, although it grows well in average soil. To keep basil growing, harvest from the top to prevent plant from going to seed. The seeds come very quickly during the growing season, so cut the plant once each week.

Use leaves in salads, vinegars, spaghetti, soups, with meat, game, fish and tomato dishes. Excellent also in flower arrangements. Basil is often used in combination with oregano, olive oil and garlic.

Summer Salad

large basil leaves
ripe tomatoes, sliced
red Italian onions, sliced
green onions, chopped
chives, chopped
1 cup honey
parsley, rosemary, chives, thyme, basil
4 cloves garlic
1/2 cup basil vinegar
sprigs of basil and green onions for garnish

Cover a platter with basil leaves. Arrange slices of tomatoes and onions so that they overlap. Spread the chopped onions and chives on top.

Add the herbs to the honey until it is thick with herbs. Mix with vinegar to make a dressing to pour over. Garnish with sprigs of basil and green onions. Hint; This salad is best when the tomatoes are really ripe and the basil leaves are crisp and prolific-late July and August at Caprilands.

Abundant Autumn

The herb garden in autumn has a special charm. Now that the competition of surrounding flower gardens is banished by the frost, the calm beauty of massed plantings of greens and greys is seen at its best. It is a time to appreciate leaf formation, texture, and the distinctive kind of growth that marks a green garden as a place for contemplation, delightful views, and mouth watering aromas.

The autumn kitchen at Caprilands is a season with many facets of interest and meaning. Modern lighting does not even completely break the spell, for the scent of the dying year is in the air and casts a curtain of magic over our tasks. Cutting a long row of sage, picking pungent pennyroyal, bunching thyme and stripping the fern-like tansy so that our garden's abundance can flavor our winter stew when this year's garden is but a fond memory in front of a fireplace.

Oregano

Oregano, also called wild marjoram, comes from the early name organy, because of its use in hot bags as an application for rheumatic swellings. It is a hardy perennial, 2 feet. Leaves are dull, gray-green and oval, with stems often purple. Flowers are pink, white, purple or lilac. The most flavorful oregano is a small-leafed, almost trailing plant with white flowers. It is easily overrun by the coarser types and needs to be kept separate and wintered inside.

Oregano prefers full sun and average garden soil, on the dry side, and always well drained. Propagate by division of established plants in the spring. Note that sowing from seeds always produces considerable variation.

Oregano leaves, fresh or dried, are used in spaghetti sauce, sparingly in salads, on tomatoes, and in herb seasoning mixtures. Excellent when combined with basil, olive oil, and garlic.

Squash Casserole

1 Hubbard or any yellow squash
1/4 teaspoon oregano
1/4 teaspoon cinnamon
butter
2 tablespoons brown sugar
1 whole nutmeg, grated
salt
pepper

Bake squash in a 350 oven until flesh is tender. Scrape flesh from shell, dot with butter and mash. Butter a casserole and fill with a layer of mashed squash. Dot with butter, sprinkle salt, pepper and oregano, cinnamon and brown sugar. Add another layer of squash and repeat spicing. Sprinkle top layer with grated whole nutmeg. Bake at 350 until flavors blend and squash warms.

Chervil

Chervil is known as the gourmet's parsley. It is an annual, 1 to 2 feet. Leaves alternate, fern-like, and spreading. The plant resembles Italian parsley, though more delicate, and turns reddish in the fall. slt has small white flowers in compound umbels.

Chervil prefers moist, well-drained soil in partial shade. Sow seeds early in spring for an early summer crop; sow again in late summer for a fall harvest and one in early spring. Self-sows year after year.

Use leaves in salads and soups, with oysters, and as a garnish. The curled variety is best to grow as it has the flavor of anise.

Chervil Soup

12 large potatoes
4 medium onions, finely chopped
1/4 teaspoon caraway seed
4 peppercorns
1/2 cup chopped fresh chervil
2 cups evaporated milk
salt
paprika

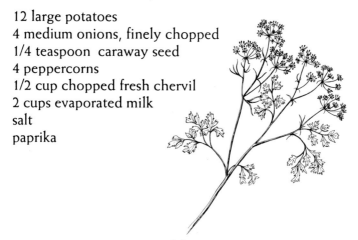

"Thompson, are you joking?"

"About this? Of course not."

"That's insane," he said. "That—that's well within the margin. Those numbers are just to give you a general sense of—God damn it, I *achieved* my goal."

"Peter," I said. "On the projects I run, numbers are numbers. I asked you here so we could talk this through and get your efficiencies up."

"A third of a percentage point? What do you want me to do? Head out to the wind farms and blow?"

"So you agree," I said, "that making up the difference wouldn't be hard to do."

I had been trying to insert some humor into the conversation, but Marcuzzi must have read my smile the wrong way.

"Honestly, Henry. Go fuck yourself."

He almost knocked over his chair as he left the room.

If I were less accustomed to this sort of friction with my colleagues, then a display of that sort would have been a minor scandal. But as it was I simply made a note to head out to Fort Collins myself at the first opportunity. I also took a deep breath and turned the C8 around on my desk so it faced me. In the cab stood a lone engineer staring ahead soberly, his little eyes taking in the seemingly endless plains to be traversed. I smiled down at the man. Yes, life wasn't easy, but luckily there was always much to be done.

I'd blocked off an hour for Marcuzzi, so now there was time to attend the meeting for the Port Oversight Committee happening down on the third floor. It was hard not to regain your confidence when you were walking with purpose through the halls of headquarters. The speckled white granite floors were always polished and glassy, while the dark wood paneling along the walls gave the place a warm, collegial air. It was early still, but the broad corridors were already resounding with the dressy heel clacks of so many agents, all of us looking sharp in our matching, agency-issued suits—navy single-button blazers with thin lapels and the option of pencil skirts for any female agents who preferred them. I passed men and women gathered in the open work areas to discuss infrastructure problems. They rearranged 3-D projections of subway tunnels and took notes while model dams buckled from the force of simulated earthquakes. A group of junior agents passed me in a huddle, grabbing fist-sized data sets from their agency phones and tossing them onto each other's screens as they argued among themselves about carbon emissions in the Rust Belt and the legalities of federal intervention.

The agency had begun seventy years back as a plucky arm of the DOT, a few dozen policy wonks who took pride in punching above their weight. But at the rate the world was urbanizing, cities had become the new space race. Our budget had exploded and we now coordinated with state and local governments to fund and advise thousands of major city improvement projects every year. We were in the middle of the golden age of American urban planning and for me the atmosphere of collective optimism never failed to produce a pleasant sense of belonging.

I remembered I had some fieldwork coming up in Wisconsin so I took out my agency phone and asked for the five-day forecast in Madison. The animation of a handsome young agent with startling blue eyes appeared on the screen.

"According to GPS," OWEN said, "you're at USMS headquarters in Suitland, Maryland."

Our chief technology engineer, Dr. Gustav Klaus, had put a lot of time and energy into OWEN's artificial intelligence interface, but the more humanlike the interface became, the more trouble I had interacting with it.

"I'll be flying out later this week, just . . ." I held the phone closer to my mouth and half barked into it, "Weather conditions. Madison, Wisconsin."

My voice was louder than expected and a fellow agent frowned at me as she passed.

"You sound stressed," OWEN said.

The animation's eyebrows arched slightly to demonstrate its concern. "While you're in Madison, you should take some time for yourself and check out Lake Monona. It's supposed to be nice."

"The weather, OWEN, I just need to know the weather."

"Oh, it's the middle of June," OWEN said. "I bet it's gorgeous."

I closed out of the interface in frustration. Between Marcuzzi and my own phone, the morning seemed off to a poor start. As I entered the meeting, I tried to focus on my eagerness to hear Agent Steinbelt's report on Norfolk and the proposed regulations the agency would attach to any new funding. Steinbelt planned to start with a virtual tour of Lambert's Point and so we were in the windowless central boardroom with one of the better 3-D projectors. I took a seat at the long conference table and told myself there was time enough for this day to be a good one. A productive one.

But almost as soon as Steinbelt brought up the simulation, the projector sputtered out and the waters that had just begun to lap at our feet faded from the room. The fire alarm let out a single shrill whoop and then went silent as our agency phones began to emit a high-pitched tone. The devices lit up the dark room as committee members removed them from their pockets and briefcases. The screens all displayed a dense block of characters:

```
!#~#K#~y1878~#@#~#!/!#~#@#y#!9!#~#@#~#!
!#~#@#~#!%!#~#@`~#!8!#~#@#~#!%!#~#`#~#!
!#~#@#~#!%!#~#@`~#!8!#~#@#~#!%!#~#`#~#!
!#~#@#~#!%!#~#@`~#!8!#~#@#~#!%!#~#`#~#!
!#~#@#~#!%!#~#@`~#!8!#~#@#~#!%!#~#`#~#!
!#@#~{LA_URBOJ_ESTAS_FROSTIGITAJ}~#!
!@^!~.>Kt&*`87@/8^8Kt%!#~#@#~9P/{788##!
!87@/~#!%!#~#@87@/~#!%!#~#@@/888Kt&*!
!@^!~.>Kt&*`87@/888Kt%!#~#@#~9P/{888##!
!#~#K#~y1878~#@#~#!/!#~#@#y#!9!#~#@#~#!
!#~#@#~#!%!#~#@`~#!8!#~#@#~#!%!#~#`#~#!
!@^!~.>Kt&*`87@/8^8Kt%!#~#@#~9P/{788##!
!87@/~#!%!#~#@87@/~#!%!#~#@@/888Kt&*!
```

I stared down at the message in confusion while the other committee members held up their phones like flashlights and shouted questions to one another.

I excused myself and hurried out of the room to report the

issue to a technician. In the hall, the sunlight coming through the windows only emphasized that the whole building had gone dark. A few nearby faces were illuminated as agents examined their phones. Elsewhere people flipped unresponsive light switches and tapped the dead call buttons on elevators. Some half leaned from their office doors as if waiting for someone to wander by with an explanation. Meanwhile, shouts began to come from behind the doors of the secure rooms whose passcode-protected entryways were sealed shut without power.

The noise from my phone grew more piercing and then abruptly stopped. I held it up to check the screen and it exploded. There was a flash of sparking blue flame and something hit my face like a fist. All at once my palm was bleeding and there was a sharp pain in my cheek. The hall was filled with the smell of burned plastic and I felt dizzy. All around me there were blurred figures stumbling forward and covering their mouths or clutching their hands to their chests. The shouts from the sealed rooms grew more frantic and I could hear people begin to pound on the doors.

My breathing felt unsteady as I removed my necktie and wrapped it around my palm. I could feel my pulse where it was hurt. When I noticed how fast it was, it went faster. There was an old panic welling up in me, a childish sense of helplessness at the world's ability to go suddenly upside down.

Something jostled me and I looked up to see a group of agents rushing past. One of them noticed me standing there and shouted, "Come on!" The urgency in his voice broke through my fear and I joined them as they dragged a desk out of the secretary pool. We used it to ram down the heavy double doors to a conference hall where we could make out people crying for help.

The rest of that day was a confusion of darkened corridors as we agents divided ourselves into groups and rushed through headquarters, prying open doors and tending to people's injuries as best we could. I eventually found the agency's director, Theodore Garrett, just outside his own office, improvising a bandage for a young woman's hand out of one of the spare dress shirts he kept in his desk. I tried to get him out of the building, but he just gave me a serious look and told me to make myself useful.

Even after the north lawn had become a frenzy of strobing lights from the arriving ambulances and fire engines, Garrett refused to leave. Around two in the morning I brought him a mug of instant coffee. He was standing under a work light in the main entryway to the first subbasement, talking a team of firefighters through a map of the floor's access tunnels. His shirtsleeves were rolled up to his elbows and he had a determined look on his face that caused even his mussed white hair to inspire confidence. The left side of my face had started to swell up from where the shards of my phone had lodged themselves and when I approached him with the coffee it seemed to take him a moment to recognize me.

When he did, he dismissed the firefighters and took my head in his hands, tilting it back so he could get a better look. He whistled the way he did when I showed him troubling data from a town where the employment rate was starting to stagnate or where the high school test scores continued to drop. It was an oddly comforting sound, indicating that things were indeed bad but it was nothing he hadn't seen before.

"Can you still see out of this one?" he said, waving a hand in front of the eye that was nearly swelled shut.

I told him I could and he stepped away.

"You'll be fine," he said, like a father playing down a scraped knee.

Strangely, it did make me feel better.

He took the mug of coffee, then thanked me. The dark hall was cluttered with upended chairs and dented waste bins. From the floor above us we could still hear shouting and the rhythmic banging of doors being smashed in.

Garrett sighed and looked down. His foot was resting on a printout bearing the cryptic block of text that had appeared on my phone. Before the building lost power this message had shown up on computer monitors all over headquarters. It was spit out again and again by copiers and printers. Garrett moved the printout right side up with the toe of his shoe and examined it.

"'La urboj estas frostigitaj.'" He recited the words slowly and then took a sip of coffee.

"What does it mean?"

He ignored the question.

"It's in Esperanto."

"You know Esperanto?"

"I don't," he said, "but I know someone who does."

o———o

Within hours, we started to hear the news coming from the city of Metropolis. While the attack on headquarters in Suitland was in progress, over three hundred miles away the agency's Metropolis station had already been burned down and its underground data center in the West Side had collapsed in on itself, leaving a building-sized sinkhole in Eleventh Avenue. Both incidents took place during the station's hours of operation and yet first responders reported no casualties at either site. Then of course there were the drones.

It didn't take our technicians long to identify that the havoc at headquarters was the result of a virus that was uploaded to the agency's supercomputer. OWEN managed most of our day-to-day operations in Suitland, everything from the building's lights and security passcodes to the automated espresso machines in the break rooms. The rest of our surveillance fleet was unaffected, but the virus had deactivated our drones over Metropolis in midflight, causing over seventy of these titanium orbs, each roughly the size of a basketball and covered in carbon-fiber strakes, to fall from the sky over the most populous city in the Western Hemisphere, crashing into buildings and wounding over a dozen people.

In the days that followed there was a fair amount of public outrage directed at the agency. Garrett accepted full liability and started arranging for the USMS to pay hospital bills and damage settlements. Despite being the director of one of the most powerful government agencies in the country, Garrett saw himself first and foremost as a public servant. He always made it clear that his driving passion in life was shortening people's commutes, haggling with zoning boards for more parks, finding the government loopholes that would send funds into the coffers of community centers and public libraries. He spoke of every city in the country with an affection and familiarity that suggested he had family there. He could tell you if the museum was any good and what parts of town to avoid after dark, where to try the pancakes and where to try the pulled pork, what kind of winter they had last year, and if it looked like the school levy was going to pass. Garrett was in his late sixties, but usually bounded around the agency like a much younger man, putting his agents to shame with his sheer exuberance. Now he was sitting in his office making call after call with his shoulders slumped and his face frozen in an expression of stunned, inarticulate grief.

I came to the agency as a civil engineer with no grasp of policy and Garrett had taken it on himself to mentor me personally. I did my best to pay back this generosity through my devotion to the agency and as a result I often found hand-drawn cartoons in our break rooms of me gingerly sniffing air from a jar labeled "Garrett's farts" or sitting in Garrett's lap as if he were a department store Santa and telling him that for Christmas I wanted a personality. But the other agents could think what they wanted. I genuinely admired the man and he was the closest I'd come to making a friend at the agency. It pained me that I had no idea how to assist or comfort him during the difficult times that were now upon us. The idea that he even needed comforting was in itself a disorienting thought.

To make matters worse, our station chief in Metropolis, Terrence Kirklin, had gone missing and was now being sought in connection to the disappearance of Sarah Laury, the mayor of Metropolis's eighteen-year-old daughter. Even with government drones raining from the sky, the news cycle was dominated by concern for Sarah, a bona fide American sweetheart. She had been a favorite of the press since her infancy. In the popular imagination, the fact that one of the most powerful families in Metropolis had adopted a child through the city's own foster system had all the charm of a fairy tale. By the time she was eight years old, the iconic photograph of her volunteering in a soup kitchen (smiling with her hair in blond ringlets, ladle filled with soup, the homeless man in the picture also smiling) was already being sold on postcards in souvenir shops in Archer Square. At age sixteen, she was on the cover of *Sports Illustrated* in the equally iconic photograph of her receiving an Olympic gold medal in individual show jumping (hair straightened, bangs, the bronze medalist looking up at her with something like awe). By seventeen, she had retired from the sport as well as a brief modeling career in order to focus on her studies and philanthropic work.

Her story had always been important to me personally. As an orphan myself, I found it encouraging to see one of my own become such a success. Though, at the agency she had recently become a bit of a controversial figure after leveling a spate of public criticisms against her father's administration and attending a few fringe political rallies throughout the city. It was unfortunate, since Mayor Laury was known for being pro-infrastructure. And now, as if her public repudiations of her own father weren't troubling enough, she had apparently taken up with a bureaucrat who was over twice her age.

Shortly after Laury went missing from the residence hall at Newton College, the young socialite uploaded a video to the internet in which she declared her love for a public servant named Terrence Kirklin. She then requested that the authorities not attempt to find her. Laury did not appear to be under duress and seemed quite sincere in her sentiments. But it wasn't long before the media started speculating that she had undergone some sort of brainwashing. This belief was most likely influenced by the fact that Sarah Laury was a blond-haired, green-eyed beauty, whereas Kirklin was known to the public only in his connection to the agency that had accidentally imploded a portion of Eleventh Avenue and sent a fleet of drones raining down over the city. Kirklin was also six foot five with a goatee and an eye patch over his right eye from an injury he had sustained in the Coast Guard. Whole television segments were devoted to the fact that he was suffering from male-pattern baldness and was perhaps a bit overweight. In person Kirklin was, though not quite handsome, a striking older man. He was tall with an intense, quiet way about him. But in the picture that the press used, Kirklin's bare scalp was shining awkwardly bright. The dark hair around his ears, usually well-groomed, was stringy and unkempt. His good eye was bloodshot and his lips were parted in a way that made him look demented.

For the agency, Kirklin's abrupt absence was a problem in itself. Certainly, everyone had always known him to be a moody and defiant station chief. His annual meetings with

Garrett were dreaded in Suitland for their tempestuousness: One year, the two got into a shouting match over optimal sidewalk width that ended with Kirklin throwing a small bookcase through the window of Garrett's office. Nevertheless, he was without question the best station chief the agency had ever seen.

For two decades he had managed the infrastructure of a city roughly the size of Rhode Island during a period of rapid and sustained growth, the population swelling to 35 million people. More electricity, water, and freight flowed in and out of Metropolis in a single day than it did in the entire state of South Dakota in six months. Kirklin's combined system of turn restrictions, one-way streets, pedestrian crosswalk intervals, street-cleaning schedules, temporary through streets, detours, bus lanes, and bike lanes was a mad symphony that allowed more people to move simultaneously across the streets of Metropolis than was ever thought possible. Kirklin liaised with every public office, utility, and public benefit corporation within the greater metro area. As a result, the city's Department of Health and Mental Hygiene reported that in the last decade life expectancy in Metropolis had increased by 2.7 years. According to the Environmental Protection Agency and the Bureau of Economic Analysis, pollution and commercial growth in the city had gone down and up, respectively. Dealing with the loss of such a man would have been a nightmare for the agency during the best of circumstances, let alone during the crisis in which we now found ourselves.

The turmoil in Metropolis and Suitland prompted our board of directors to form an oversight committee that put the majority of our projects on hold while they conducted an audit of Garrett's leadership. Already they were trying to keep any investigation of the cyberattack private despite Garrett's requests for outreach to the FBI. After the PR disaster of the crashing drones, they were anxious to keep any details of the attack from getting picked up by the press as a potential data breach. When these severe-looking men and women weren't interrogating Garrett, they could be seen wandering through headquarters, taking in all of the fallout from the attack with colicky disapproval.

Garrett asked me to meet with him in his office later that week, and I expected a war council of sorts, an urgent discussion on how to defend the agency against the destructive influence of the oversight committee. As I took my usual seat, I noticed on his desk one of the printouts with the block of text produced by the virus. After Garrett had tipped me off about the line in Esperanto, I'd typed it into a translation engine, which rendered it as: "The cities are frozen." A vague threat or warning I didn't understand. Before I could ask him about it, he told me the committee had instructed him to step down as director by the end of the month.

For a moment the floor attempted to switch places with the ceiling, but I surprised myself by rising from my seat and saying with confidence, "No."

Garrett looked up at me with a question on his face.

"I can put together a dissent channel," I said. "Give me some time to write the memo."

"Sit down."

"I know the agents don't like me, sir, but everyone will sign it if they know it's for you."

He waved me off.

"Henry, if there's so much as a whiff of opposition, they'll gut this place. Do you understand?"

"Without you, this agency—"

"Stop," Garrett said. "We're talking about an irreparable loss of institutional memory. Not just the people who sign that memo. Anyone who's ever sat in on a meeting with you is out the door. The agency as you know it will be finished."

I was standing in front of his desk. I wanted to leave and put together that memo without delay, but didn't see how I could without his permission.

"Sir, what am I supposed to do?"

He looked up at me until I sat back down.

"You don't want to hear this," he said, "but their decision makes sense. You don't have all the facts."

I asked him what the facts were and he told me not to get ahead of him. He then surprised me by taking a pack of cigarettes from his desk and offering me one.

"This is a federal building, sir."

Garrett laughed and wagged a finger as if he thought I might say that, then lit the cigarette with a book of matches from his blazer pocket. I'd never seen him smoke before and the tobacco smelled stale.

"Do you remember an agent named Stuart Biggs?" he said.

I did. He'd been an undistinguished agent in Sewerage with a geekish demeanor that was extreme even for the agency. In other words, he had as few friends as I did. When I was alone with him in the elevators he once told me, apropos of nothing, that a lifelong dream of his was to revolutionize sewer systems using electric turbines he called waste mills.

"Bit of an odd duck," I said.

Garrett nodded.

"I suppose that's why no one noticed he was reassigned to Metropolis eight months ago."

Garrett took another pull on his cigarette and let me take in this detail. Kirklin never accepted transfers from Suitland because he assumed the agent in question would be sent by Garrett to keep tabs on him. He liked to recruit his agents from Metropolis, specifically from programs for troubled youths, a stark contrast to the tweedy men and women that composed Garrett's core staff in Suitland. My first two years at the agency, I had sent in requests every few weeks for permission to contribute to various projects being run in Metropolis. After my twentieth rejection, I received a note on Kirklin's letterhead asking me to tell Garrett he said hello.

"That seems strange given Kirklin's paranoia."

"He wasn't paranoid," Garrett said. "I was spying on him."

Garrett put his cigarette in the side of his mouth and pulled a file folder as thick as a phone book from a shelf behind him. He seemed to admire its heft before dropping it onto his desk.

"Whenever I tried to sneak candidates directly through Kirklin's recruitment process, he'd end up having them shadow his interns. So last year I entered Biggs into the station assignment pool with an internal note that I didn't think he was right for policy work. Kirklin hired him a week later. Since then I've had Biggs monitor Kirklin's behavior to report on anything strange."

He pointed to the file folder on his desk.

"This is January to February of this year."

"Biggs was comfortable with this?"

"He was excited to work in Metropolis. I also approved some sewerage project in Tucson for him. I thought he was going to do a cartwheel on his way out. But now he's gone quiet along with the rest of Kirklin's people. We need someone to make contact with him. The attacks in Metropolis and on headquarters are connected and I think Biggs might know enough to convince the board to open our investigation to outside law enforcement."

Garrett ashed his cigarette into a mug bearing the agency's seal. I didn't appreciate the gesture, but I told myself that these were difficult times. He wasn't himself.

"That means I need someone in Metropolis," he said. "It has to be someone I trust, because the board can't know I'm going around them on this. And this Biggs thing has to be worked fast. Because whatever this is"—he held up the printout of Esperanto—"it isn't over."

I started to understand why I was sitting there. Despite my unpopularity, I knew the staff at headquarters down to the mailroom. Every once in a while Garrett liked me to help him pull a name for an assignment. To find Biggs he'd need an agent with experience in the field and enough discretion to keep the board from finding out, but one young enough to be unphased knocking on strange doors for an out-and-out goose chase. It'd be tough putting together my recommendations on such short notice. And with the board challenging projects left and right, no one was going to want to leave their desks until they were sure their portfolios were safe.

enjoy the hospitality of Friends Forever Dumpling House while I found a real room uptown. It was early still and there was enough time for me to swing by the transit museum to get my picture with the Steam Beetle before starting the hunt for Biggs.

From downstairs came the sound of Bao-yu yelling and slamming the front door.

"That could be trouble," OWEN said. "I'll see if I can get satellite visual on the street out front."

"Sure," I said, giving that preposterous room one last look and trying to decide if I wanted to walk to the museum or get myself pumped up for it by taking the subway.

OWEN looked up at the ceiling in concentration and I took the opportunity to reopen the top drawer of the bureau. I pulled off the tie clip and wrapped it tightly in one of the pairs of underwear before dropping it into the drawer. I shut the bureau and turned around just in time to see OWEN flicker out of sight. His voice was still able to move about the room, but was so muffled that his confused and urgent protests were barely discernible.

Bao-yu's shouting continued downstairs and was now accompanied by a loud banging. I grabbed my bag and hat as I made my way to the stairs. In the foyer, I found Bao-yu with her hands pressed flat against the front door, shouting at whoever was pounding on the other side. The door shook violently with each blow and Bao-yu leaned in as if to bolster it.

I was just asking her if everything was all right when the tip of an axe blade poked through the door. She screamed at the sight of it and fled up the stairs back into 2G. The door received two more massive thwacks before it collapsed into the foyer in a heap.

Standing outside were two men dressed in matching suits, which I was surprised to notice were the USMS cut. The men could have been mistaken for field agents except that their suits were black instead of the usual navy and they weren't wearing fedoras. The bigger one must have been at least six foot, five inches and had a thick beard as well as blond hair that came to his shoulders. He stood holding his axe at the ready and looking down at the demolished door as if to intimidate it into further submission. The other one was leaning forward as he brushed splinters and dust from the broken door off his pant legs. When he stood up and adjusted his thin black tie, it occurred to me with surprise that I was looking at Stuart Biggs.

As soon as he spotted me he tilted his head back and smiled, showing a mouth of large, perfectly white teeth.

"Henry Thompson," he said, "as I live and breathe."

"Stuart?"

He spoke rapidly to his companion in an odd-sounding language.

"Sorry, Henry," he said. "Nothing personal."

The blond man grunted in response and stepped toward me, lifting his axe. I fell back into the stairs as he took a wide, heavy swing, the axe blade narrowly missing my head and sinking into the wall.

I scrambled up the stairs as he started to tug the axe free, and it wasn't long before I heard them both heading up after me, their pace slow and deliberate.

On the third floor, I slipped into my room, shut the door, and began digging through my travel bag for my new cell phone. Once I found it I got down on the floor and did a quick army crawl under the bed. Luckily, OWEN had gone quiet in the drawer and I was hopeful that it would take the two men a while to find me hiding under the sagging twin bed.

When I hit the phone's power button, the screen lit up with a series of loud-but-welcoming chimes before asking me to register my Newtech mobile device.

Below I could hear the footfalls of the two men making their way up the stairs as they talked to one another in their foreign tongue. Their tone was casual; they could have been discussing anything from baseball to their plans for that night once they had finished killing me.

I pressed the button indicating that I did not want to register my phone. An hourglass appeared, rotated, and then disappeared before a message flashed onto the screen: "You must register in order to use your Newtech mobile device."

It sounded like the two men were walking down the third-floor hallway, smashing things indiscriminately as they went.

The phone asked me for my preferred username. I pushed random keys on the screen's keyboard until I had entered the required number of characters. When I hit submit the resulting text was autocorrected to "Salad daughter urine gut."

The hourglass reappeared and rotated. A new message: "The username Salad daughter urine gut is not available. Please select any one of the following usernames: Urine_Daughter912, GutSalad727, Daughter_Gut613!, _SaladUrine4, Daughter_Salad212, or Gut_Urine474."

I selected Gut_Urine474 and was immediately prompted to create a password. I mashed the keyboard again and hit enter, prompting another message: "This password is weak. Are you sure you would like to continue?" I selected yes.

The men's voices sounded close.

The hourglass reappeared and was followed by a flashing screen that congratulated me on registering and asked me to reenter my password. In the same moment, the door to the room flew off its hinges. The blond man pulled me out from under the bed by my ankle and rolled me onto my back.

Biggs stood in the doorway with his hands in his pockets. My phone had fallen to the floor and the blond man crushed it under his heel before raising his axe as if to bring the handle down onto my face. I instinctively brought my leg up and kicked, planting my heel into the man's crotch as hard as I could. He dropped the axe and fell to his knees.

Biggs gasped at the sight of his partner on the floor. He ran to his side and began to rub his shoulders.

"Spiru," he said. "Spiru."

I grabbed the axe as I stood up and held it in front of me, more as a partition than a weapon.

"Biggs, what's going on?" I said.

He turned to me as he continued rubbing his partner's shoulders, his eyes wide with anger and righteous disbelief.

"Can you give us a minute? Can you?! You kicked Teddy right in the testicles, which is a pretty cheap shot."

I was taken aback by the anger in his voice. There was also something strange about his enunciation that I didn't recall from our interactions at headquarters, a slight sibilance that wasn't quite a lisp.

"He was going to hit me with an axe."

"Yeah, with the handle," he said. "You would have been fine."

"He—on the stairs, he swung the blade at me."

"So he got carried away a few minutes ago. Does that mean he deserves to be kicked in the nuts for the rest of his life?"

Teddy moaned at the mention of his testicles. When he winced, baring his teeth, I noticed that his too were incredibly white.

"You mean you're not trying to kill me?"

"Not *here*," he said, sounding irritated. "We're supposed to throw you off the Lennox Street Bridge."

I was still unsure whether I was prepared to hit someone with an axe when Teddy rose to his feet with the pained expression of an athlete who knew he would be expected to tough it out. He took a deep breath and stepped in a slow circle, looking for his axe. As soon as he noticed I was holding it, he took a few steps forward and unceremoniously punched me in the face, taking it from me as easily as if I had handed it to him. I stumbled back toward the bed and Biggs resumed his position near the door, watching the proceedings with a look of grim satisfaction that suggested I probably wouldn't make it to Lennox Street.

Teddy lifted the axe and gave it another broad, heavy swing in my direction. I fell back onto the bed, which collapsed under me—making the blade land too high. As Teddy once again struggled to pull his axe from the wall I kicked him in the crotch a second time. The look of astonishment on his face was indescribable.

Biggs rushed forward and lifted me by my collar, then hit me in the mouth and threw me into the bureau, which splintered beneath me. The underwear came spilling out and I saw the tie clip slide across the floor.

Biggs wrenched the axe out of the wall and looked ready to bring it down on me himself, but suddenly OWEN appeared in the doorway and shouted for everyone to freeze. He was holding a samurai sword, which he leveled at Biggs.

"Drop the axe," OWEN said. "It's the nerd or your life."

He chopped the air with his sword and his interface produced a simultaneous whistling sound that was a little too loud to be realistic, though neither of the men seemed to notice. Biggs tossed the axe to the floor and put his hands up. Teddy was still on the ground and had to push himself up to his knees before following suit.

OWEN gestured for me to stand up, then ordered the two men to sit in the middle of the floor with their backs together.

"All right, Thompson," he said, pretending to be careful as he slid his sword into the scabbard hanging from his belt. "Tie them up."

Having just narrowly escaped a beheading, I found it difficult to match OWEN's poise.

"With what?"

"Oh, I don't know," he said, his voice taking on a certain sharpness as he pointed toward the demolished bureau. "How about some of those disgusting pairs of underwear over there."

"Or," Biggs chimed in, "you could use our ties."

OWEN silenced him by pulling his sword a few inches from its scabbard and slamming it back down.

I tied their hands behind their backs and noticed that their fingertips looked as if they had been burned. OWEN noticed it too and tried to ask the men about it. Teddy kept his head bowed in silent prayer over his genitals and Biggs just laughed, saying that they'd both been doing some ironing.

"How did you find us?" OWEN said.

"This is our city," Biggs answered. "No one sets foot here without us knowing."

"Who's us?" I asked.

OWEN shook his head like I'd just embarrassed him, then took a step toward Biggs.

"Where's Kirklin?"

Biggs smiled.

"Kirklin who?"

OWEN unsheathed the katana and raised it over his head before letting out a blood-curdling howl. He kept the sword overhead for a moment, observing Biggs for any sign that his resolve had been weakened. When Biggs only looked confused, OWEN frowned and put the sword away again.

He told me to get my things together and stepped out into the hallway before adding, "And don't forget your tie clip."

I stooped to pick up the clip and felt a sharp pinch in my back as well as a stiffness in my calf from when I'd been thrown through the bureau.

"Wait a second," I said, trying not to limp as I followed him into the hallway. I waved him away from the door and lowered my voice.

"Can you contact the police or something?"

"No," he said, crossing his arms in front of his chest.

"But aren't you, like, a . . ."

"Technological marvel capable of contacting every single police station in the world in one-billionth of the time it would take you to fall down a flight of stairs?"

"Yes?"

"You're right, but I'm not calling the cops."

When I asked him why not, he shrugged.

"Oh, a couple reasons," OWEN said. "First of all, on the plane you insulted my disguises and when I told you that my feelings were hurt you persisted in being rude."

I started to stammer out something in my defense, but OWEN cut me off.

"And when those goons showed up, I couldn't do anything about it because you put me in a drawer, and judging from the smashed, low-end cell phone in there I'm guessing when you needed help I wasn't even your first choice. So while I am obligated to help you get out of here alive, I'm not going to be taking orders from someone whose attitude is so completely toxic and unhelpful."

There was an awkward silence between us before I came out with the only thing I could think to say, even though it felt absurd saying it to a computer. "OWEN, I'm sorry."

He considered my apology a little while before accepting it.

"Wonderful," I said. "Can you call the police now?"

"No."

I took a deep breath. Keeping OWEN's apparent vulnerability in mind, I felt it was probably for the best that I remain calm.

"Why not?"

"Well," OWEN said, "I still don't really feel like it, because that was a terrible apology. Also, we were sent to the city to find out what Biggs knows, which we can't do if he's in custody. And lastly, according to police scanners, Bao-yu called 911 about seven minutes ago. So get your bag, get Biggs, and let's get out of here."

Biggs and Teddy had left a black Buick sedan at an angle in the middle of the street with its engine still running. OWEN's sword kept Biggs docile while I popped the trunk and loaded him inside. Once I was behind the wheel, I saw OWEN standing by the passenger-side door. He shoved his sword up the sleeve of his jacket, then cleared his throat. I followed his eyes down to a black soft leather briefcase on the passenger seat. I had to stare at it for a moment before I understood. I threw the briefcase into the back and he appeared in the seat next to me as I straightened the car out and pulled off down the street.

○———○

OWEN directed me to Velmer Hill, a dozen blocks of high-end office and residential buildings in the West Side. Taking a nervous right onto Quillent Street, I asked OWEN what in the hell was going on and why he had been asking Biggs about Terrence Kirklin. He glanced back toward the trunk and projected his voice into my ear as a whisper.

"Keep your voice down," he said. "And if you'd listened to me on the plane, you'd already know."

OWEN used satellite imaging to confirm no drones were

following us. He also managed to locate a federally owned building in the area that was closed for the day, its empty rooftop parking lot ideal for an interrogation. As we pulled up, I saw a large brass placard over its main entrance identifying it as the regional office of our colleagues at the United States Census Bureau. The agency enjoyed a good relationship with the USCB and so I was reluctant to follow OWEN's suggestion to ram through the steel security gate blocking the ramp to the building's roof. Only after he promised to help allocate $6,500 of agency funds to reimburse them did I finally rev the engine and plow through the gate, sending it sparking up the ramp in a twisted heap.

When we reached the roof, I drove through the lot to the far row of spaces marked for visitor parking. As I navigated our stolen Buick neatly between the painted lines of Visitor Parking 0001, OWEN looked around at the empty lot.

"You know," he said, "sometimes you exhibit what a psychologist might call 'internalized oppression.'"

"What's that supposed to mean?"

But he had already projected himself out into the lot, where he was peering over the roof's barrier wall down into the street. Even though he must have been using a combination of infrared, sonar, and satellite imaging to check if anyone had noticed us breaking past the building's security gate, the projection of OWEN was looking down into the street with a large pair of binoculars and occasionally licking his index finger to test the wind.

When he was satisfied we wouldn't be disturbed, he returned to the passenger seat and regarded me for a moment before again projecting his voice softly into my ear: "We have to interrogate him now. Are you up to it?" I hesitated before telling him I was. "You might have to punch him. Do you know how to punch people?" I thought for a moment, then shook my head no. OWEN shrugged as if to suggest he hadn't thought so and brought up an animation that hovered above the dashboard. It depicted a man's face opposite a floating, disembodied fist. Flashing arrows highlighted the fact that the thumb was curled outside the fist and that the impact should fall on the first two knuckles. There was a series of quick diagrams on appropriate stance and follow-through; then the fist began slamming into the man's face again and again, a thumbs-up icon appearing at the center of each impact. I held my clenched fist up to OWEN to demonstrate my form and he examined it for a moment before projecting a thumbs-up icon onto it.

"Are you ready?" OWEN said.

I nodded, then stared blankly at OWEN.

"You have to get out of the car and open the trunk," he said.

"Right," I said. "Sorry."

As we walked to the back of the car, something occurred to me. I took a few steps away from the trunk and lowered my voice.

"OWEN, are you going to pull out a samurai sword again?"

"Absolutely," he said, stepping away from the car himself and half pulling the sword from his sleeve as if he were trying to reassure me.

"Why a sword?"

"I told you," he said, taking the sword the rest of the way

out and slicing the air with it as he spoke. "I'm a Kurosawa fan. The katana is an elegant weapon."

"OWEN, did Klaus ever show you *The Magnificent Seven*?"

He lowered the sword and gave my question some thought, eventually snapping his fingers.

"You think a gun would be scarier?"

I nodded and he looked down at his sword briefly before whipping it off the roof.

"Okay, I'll try it," he said. "Also, can I just say? I really appreciate how you communicated that feedback. When you locked me in that drawer I started to feel pretty low, so I read through some of the self-help books available online. I finished about eighty thousand, and more than half of them suggested that discussion and compromise are the lifeblood of a successful relationship, whether personal or professional."

I told him that seemed perfectly interesting, but he ignored me when I tried to remind him of the bound man in our trunk.

"I read a book called *Excuse You*," he said. "It mentioned that it's important to be clear and honest when someone has hurt your feelings. That's what I always do, because I have what the book calls 'healthy impulses.' But it also said you need to communicate clearly when someone has behaved in a way that makes you feel valued and respected. So that's what I'm doing right now, Henry."

OWEN paused and then said expansively, "I'm communicating that to you."

"That's great," I said. "Maybe we can talk about this some more after we've interrogated Biggs."

"Oh, definitely, I'd like that," he said, sounding excited by the possibility of further discussion. "Also, if we have time later maybe I could summarize the compare-and-contrast essay Gus had me write on Sturges and Kurosawa. He said I managed to draw some very subtle parallels."

I wondered whether OWEN might actually be a more effective partner when he was upset with me, but I settled on telling him that sounded fun as I moved toward the trunk.

I opened it and inside Biggs was lying perfectly still, staring up at us without expression. Once I pulled him from the trunk, he stood behind the car, looking off into the middle distance with fatalistic resignation, as if he understood he was in danger but simply wasn't impressed by the fact. I took his elbow and jostled him, drawing his attention to OWEN, who was standing across from us.

"Henry just learned how to punch people," OWEN said. "He couldn't be more excited to give it a try. But if you answer our questions, I can make sure it doesn't come to that."

Biggs looked over his shoulder at the view of the city behind us and OWEN snapped to get his attention. When that didn't work, he pulled a gun from inside his jacket and cocked it. Biggs turned to face him, slow but obedient. I was discouraged to see that the gun OWEN had chosen was a pearl-handled Smith & Wesson that looked at least a hundred years old.

Already the interrogation was going poorly and I was dreading the possibility that I might have to punch someone.

"I'll start with an easy one," OWEN said. "Where is Terrence Kirklin?"

Biggs shook his head once and then smiled with his disturbingly bright teeth.

OWEN motioned for me to hit him. I steadied myself by grabbing his shoulder and brought my fist back a little too far, but otherwise I was pleased with how I carried the whole thing off. The punch landed squarely against his jaw with what felt like substantial force. However, the sense of relief I felt at having successfully followed OWEN's instructions was quickly replaced by horror when I saw that Biggs's teeth had come out. Not individually. All of them, together. His full set of teeth clacked once on the pavement and then fell in two halves, straight and shining, connected to a pair of glistening pink gums. The unexpected sight caused me to shriek briefly, but OWEN was fascinated. He bent down on one knee to examine them before calling out, "They're dentures."

Biggs stood with tendrils of drool hanging from his soft, empty mouth.

His words were slurred when he spoke, but I was able to make out, "Not bad for a first punch."

"Interesting," OWEN said, still examining the teeth. "No fingerprints. No dental records."

He looked up at Biggs and said, "You're staying right here until we know everything. I can have Henry work on you all day if that's the way you want it. Or you can end this now and save yourself the discomfort."

Biggs seemed to consider OWEN's threat for a moment before shrugging to himself and head-butting me in the

When I was a little boy my mother always told me
Way haul away, we'll haul away, Joe!
That if I did not kiss the girls my lips would all
  grow moldy.
First I met a Spanish girl, who said that I was lazy.
Way haul away, we'll haul away, Joe!
Then I met a Yankee girl—

Before he could finish the verse, he heaved again and the words landed with a wet splat into the garbage can—"Whose blond hair drove me crazy." They lingered there for a few seconds and then faded into nothing just when a thought occurred to me that managed to transcend my own inebriation. OWEN had just coughed up perhaps Kirklin's only weakness, the one aspect of his recent behavior in which he didn't seem to be in complete control of himself and everyone around him. *A Yankee girl whose blond hair drove me crazy.* If Kirklin was still in the city, it stood to reason his girlfriend was too.

7 Before her alleged kidnapping, Sarah Laury was a rising sophomore at Newton College, a private school tucked away in Barington Heights. It was the North Side's wealthiest neighborhood, with its lush, flowered medians, sidewalks peopled by elderly women in furs, and doormen in epauletted blazers and flat black-billed caps. OWEN and I couldn't have looked more out of place that Monday morning as we marched, hungover, up Telmont Avenue toward the Newton campus.

My other clothes were still in the model tenement, so I'd had to sleep in my suit at the YMCA, where OWEN and I had passed the night. OWEN had lain facedown on the linoleum floor of our room with his arms at his sides, shifting only twice to vomit into the plastic garbage bin at the foot of my bed. In the morning I'd had to give the tie clip a few hard flicks to rouse him. He was upset at first, but once I explained my plan to find Kirklin through Sarah Laury he was on his feet and full of questions.

"How is this supposed to help?" he said, straightening his hair and changing his suit in our room's small mirror. "The whole city has been looking for her since she ran off."

"We don't need to find her," I said. "We just need to learn more about her. Laury's video went live the night before Kirklin attacked headquarters. That was an unnecessary risk Kirklin either allowed or couldn't prevent. So if we're looking for loose ends, Laury seems like a good place to start."

OWEN stopped fussing with his tie and gave this some thought.

"Human beings *are* weird when it comes to love," he admitted. "I read an article the other day about a woman in Houston who tried to marry her pet turtle."

This comment hung in the air for a moment. But I was eager to get him on board, so I agreed enthusiastically, at which point he started to talk about the plan as if it were his idea.

It took him only a few seconds to analyze every feature article ever written on the subject of Sarah Laury. As I washed my face in the public restroom at the Y, OWEN stood over my shoulder and summarized what he felt were some of his more interesting findings:

- Sarah Laury was a vegan for ethical reasons.
- She'd described herself in over twenty-three different interviews as an avid reader.
- Her dislikes included lack of intellectual curiosity, institutional racism, and cilantro.
- The previous year she'd organized a fund-raiser for the victims of a hospital fire in Baton Rouge. The cell phone footage of her playing "When the Saints Go Marching In" on her trumpet had gone viral and spurred a brief trumpeting fad.
- She was an assistant editor at Newton's literary journal, *The Newton Quarterly Review*, and was also a staff

writer for the school's newspaper, *The Marigold*, to which she contributed a monthly column.

- This spring she had played Nathan Detroit in the drama department's all-female production of *Guys and Dolls*.
- Around the same time, she'd starred in an avant-garde play that she had written and directed herself.

OWEN also brought up an interview that had originally been conducted by a reporter for the online edition of *Metropolis News*, but which had been reposted to a blog called *Real Celebrity Meltdowns*. It was from over a year ago and showed Laury conservatively dressed and seated across from a young male journalist, discussing an event she was planning for the Metropolis Food Bank. After a few polite questions regarding the benefit, the journalist asked her whether she could address the rumors that she was considering breast augmentation.

Laury's smile vanished and she turned a shade of red that seemed more angry than embarrassed. She looked as if she were about to ask the man what on earth he was talking about, but instead stammered for a moment.

"I'm talking about people," she finally managed to say, "people starving to death less than a mile from where we're sitting right now, and you're asking if I have any future plans for my breasts?"

Her voice was calm but incredulous.

"I'm sorry, Ms. Laury," the reporter said, doing his best to project an air of professional obligation onto his question, "but these rumors exist and I have a responsibility."

"Oh, yes," Laury said. "It must be awful for you, having to answer to every thirteen-year-old boy on the internet."

"So," the reporter said, pushing ahead, "there's no truth to the rumors?"

"Actually, there is," she said, pointing at the reporter. "I'm about to have this tit removed right now."

She turned to someone off camera and soon a well-dressed older woman with a clipboard informed the man that the interview was over. Before the video ended there was one last shot of the reporter as he prepared to leave the room, his expression a convincing attempt at bewilderment. Though, his slight smile showed that he had gotten exactly what he had hoped to out of Sarah Laury.

When the video ended, OWEN turned to me and said, "Seven million views."

I shook my head. No teenager should have been expected to cope with such a perverse level of attention. And while her apparent attachment to Kirklin remained a mystery, it was obvious to me why she might have been eager to withdraw so dramatically from public life.

This sad insight made it that much more awkward when OWEN and I concluded that, since her interests at Newton seemed mostly literary, the next logical step in our investigation was to steal a copy of her library records, which OWEN was unable to access remotely on account of the school's outdated computer system.

Now it was barely seven in the morning and I was walking through one of the richest neighborhoods in the world wearing a wrinkled suit that stunk of stale booze. After a while I caught OWEN regarding me with what looked like concern and I asked him if everything was all right. He paused in an obvious effort to phrase something carefully, then said, "Last night—after the bar."

"Yeah?"

"You talked about model trains a lot."

"Oh."

"Like, a lot a lot."

I had no memory of discussing my hobby with OWEN and was wondering what I could have said.

"I collect them."

"Henry, I know."

"Sorry," I said. "It was just because—"

OWEN's expression froze at what he seemed to expect would be more train talk.

"I'll keep the train stuff to myself," I said.

"Not forever," OWEN said. "I just think I've hit my limit for this trip."

This conversation was luckily interrupted when an older woman passing by with her corgi took in our messy appearance and abruptly crossed to the other side of the street. I shot OWEN a meaningful glance and he nodded in agreement before turning us into a pair of well-dressed older women. The disguises proved effective, earning us half a dozen friendly greetings from various doormen as we continued up the avenue. When we walked up to the gates of Newton's campus, OWEN gave the young guard in the security booth a matronly frown and he waved apologetically, buzzing us in.

All schools in the city had suspended classes in the wake

of the attacks. Newton was no exception, its campus deserted and quiet except for the snapping of a flag at half-mast in the middle of the main quad. This sound was joined by our footsteps as we followed the paved paths that led to the school's library.

It was a three-story brick building, which sat between a mostly empty faculty parking lot and a large stone-lined pond surrounded by willow trees and wooden benches. We had assumed the library would be closed and had been hoping to sneak in through a window, but as we approached we saw that the building's lights were on and there was movement inside. OWEN paused for a moment to consider this, then turned us both into firemen and headed toward the library's entrance without explanation.

The rattle of our oxygen tanks and gear filled the place as we entered. The first floor of the library was a charming space filled with round worktables and warmly lit study nooks furnished with overstuffed leather chairs. It was empty except for a middle-aged woman in a red turtleneck who was sorting books on a handcart behind the front counter. She looked understandably alarmed when she saw us. OWEN gave me a reassuring smile, then turned to the woman and screamed, "FIRE! FIRE! FIRE! GET OUT OF HERE!"

She gasped and grabbed a cardigan off the back of a chair before half running to the exit. As she pushed her way through the door she glanced over her shoulder at OWEN, who made an aggressive shooing motion, at which point she dropped her sweater and broke into an all-out sprint toward the parking lot. OWEN vanished and reappeared standing behind the counter. He looked around the empty library and screamed the word "Fire!" a few more times, scanning for any movement before turning back to me.

"Lock the door," he said.

I walked over to the double doors and turned the dead bolt.

"Couldn't you have lied about something else?"

OWEN gave me a long, blank look, as if by asking this question I had betrayed a fundamental lack of understanding with respect to the intensity of his hangover.

"I just wanted to get her out of here before you tried to kick her in the genitals," he said.

He then waved his hand lazily in the direction of a wire rack of periodicals near the front door, which became engulfed in flames.

"There," he said. "A fire. Now come over here and help me with this thing."

He was frowning at the large tube monitor and tower of the library's primitive computer.

"What are they spending these kids' tuition on?" he said, running his hand along the bulky monitor. "This old girl should be enjoying her retirement somewhere."

I waggled the mouse and the computer sprang noisily to life. Their user database wasn't password protected, so I was able to pull up Laury's library records without any trouble. I clicked print and an old line printer on the counter began to churn out her borrowing history on continuous paper.

I was then startled by a pounding coming from the library's entrance. The security guard from the main gate was pressing his forehead against the glass with his hands cupped around his eyes, while the librarian stood behind him, peering over his shoulder and holding her recovered sweater to her chest. OWEN and I were still disguised as firemen, though the sight of us standing behind the counter watching a document print must have for all practical purposes blown our cover.

OWEN lit up the entire counter with more fake flames and put them out with a fire extinguisher. He waved authoritatively for the guard and librarian to back away from the building, but the guard only squinted at him for a moment before banging on the door again and shouting for us to unlock it.

"Okay," OWEN said, lowering his fire extinguisher. "Put the tie clip near a window and I'll distract them. Just let me know when you have what you need."

I pulled off the clip and headed toward the front windows, where I placed it on the sill. I was barely halfway back to the counter when my fireman disguise disappeared and I heard the guard and librarian begin to scream, the sound becoming gradually softer as whatever monster OWEN had conjured chased them toward the parking lot.

He had bought me some time, so I decided to see what else I could find on Laury in the library's computer by searching the catalog for any of her student writing. Dozens of hits came up for her contributions to *The Marigold*, bound issues of which were kept in the periodical section on the second floor. There was also a listing in the library's drama section for the play she had written.

My hangover was gaining on me and I was pouring boozy sweat by the time I made it upstairs to *The Marigold*'s archive. I pulled the most recent volumes off the shelf, then grabbed the bound manuscript of her play from the drama section.

From outside there was a loud roar and more screaming. I tucked the books under my arm and moved to the window at the end of the stacks to see how OWEN was doing. Given his performance at the museum, I was surprised that he had only turned himself into a bear. Granted, the appearance of a 1,500-pound Kodiak bear in the middle of a city campus was strange, but compared to a clown monster, the choice of bear attack was at least beginning to approach the outer realms of subtlety. OWEN had scared the librarian and guard up onto the roof of a Honda Civic. The two held each other and wept while OWEN paced around the car with his mouth foaming.

Across the parking lot I spotted a large dormitory and realized that, while comparatively understated, OWEN's bear was most likely drawing too much attention. I rushed back down to the lobby, where I attempted to leap over the front counter to retrieve Laury's borrowing history. Instead my shoe caught on one of the computer cables and I fell over the counter, pulling the old monitor and tower down onto the floor with me. My other foot winged a metal shelf filled with reserved books. It teetered precariously for a moment before falling back and knocking over another shelf behind it.

Once I'd gotten up and dusted myself off, I tore Laury's record from the printer. I retrieved the tie clip on my way out the door and told OWEN it was time to go. He projected his voice into my ear, telling me to make my way to the front gate. Halfway there, OWEN's roars died down and I saw that he was running alongside me. At the campus entrance, I entered the empty guard booth and opened the gates. Just then a truck from Metropolis Animal Control pulled up the main drive and OWEN waved it through. The driver slowed as he passed us and rolled down his window, asking us for directions to the school's library. OWEN, wearing a guard uniform, told him where to go, then thanked him, letting him know he had showed up just in time.

———○———

We headed down toward Berkshire Square in the Lower North Side, where the air of forbidding privilege eventually gave way to a modicum of economic diversity. Boutique clothing stores stood next to barber shops and Dominican cafés. Banks and business-class hotels overlooked the stretch of sidewalk near the entrance of Berkshire Square Park where men and women sat next to folding tables, selling handmade jewelry and amateur oil paintings. Despite the sense of unease that hung over the city, plenty of citizens had chosen to go about their business. The young guardsman standing with a rifle next to the bluestone basin of the park's massive, thudding fountain was an ominous sight, but it didn't stop a young couple from having a loud argument near the benches on the park's high terrace or the busker from playing the violin while balancing a leashed tabby cat on his head.

A few more blocks and we found a small diner, which

seemed like a fine place to go over our haul. Inside, the air smelled savory and half-burned, every surface stained a warm sepia from decades of hash brown smoke. We took one of the cracked vinyl booths in back. A young woman who'd been watching the news on a small television behind the lunch counter appeared next to our table. She kept glancing back at the television and there was a heaviness in her voice when she asked for our order.

Her obvious grief over the attacks made our presence feel like an intrusion, and so I tried to sound apologetic when I asked for a cup of coffee and an omelet. She then looked to OWEN, who was absently smacking his lips as he looked over the laminated menu doubling as a place mat. Regardless of the fact that he was incapable of eating, he ordered himself two plates of onion rings, a stuffed pepper, and a Fresca. I tried to suggest that he and I could share my omelet, but the woman had already made off with our order.

OWEN turned to me, pleased.

"I've never ordered food before," he said.

He was in a pleasant mood so this seemed like a good opportunity to provide him with some constructive criticism regarding his behavior at the library. I told him it was important to remember that we were both public servants and that no matter how desperate the situation we should do our best to proceed with a certain amount of professionalism and decency, especially since this was such a frightening time for the city.

"What are you talking about?"

"You screamed 'fire' at a librarian," I said. "You made

her think she was about to be mauled by a bear. And after all that, she's going to find the place trashed."

"Wait a minute," OWEN said. "Who trashed the library?"

"Well, I mean, I did, because you—"

OWEN leaned over the table, his eyes huge with mock outrage.

"Henry, why did you do that?"

"You were drawing too much attention to us, so I was in a hurry. Some shelves got knocked over."

"That was a *library*, Henry. For *students*."

"Cut it out."

He held out his hands to show he was now being serious.

"All right," he said, "so the takeaway is next time you shouldn't rush. Running in an unfamiliar setting is dangerous. Speaking as your friend, I'm just glad you didn't get hurt. But as far as my bear projection is concerned, I think you're being a little narrow-minded. Those people should be thanking me for getting their minds off all the terrorism."

Our drinks arrived and OWEN nodded his thanks to the waitress, who didn't seem to notice that he was now wearing a ten-gallon cowboy hat. She placed the coffee and Fresca on the table without comment and returned to the kitchen.

"That's exactly the sort of thing I'm talking about," I said. "Completely unnecessary. If we're going to stop Kirklin we need to focus."

"I don't think so," OWEN said. "Kirklin has the market cornered on the kind of focus you're talking about. If we act like well-behaved USMS agents, he's going to get away with whatever it is he's after. We need to be as ridiculous as possible."

A stubborn silence settled between us. He adjusted the cowboy hat on his head, making a big show of the fact that his hands were now lobster claws.

"Okay," I said. "Point taken."

"Is it?"

OWEN tilted his head back and began pushing a mustache out of his upper lip. In a matter of seconds it was touching the table. He curled the ends of it with his claws.

"Okay, okay," I said. "You win."

He clunked his claws together in celebration and took on his normal shape just in time to receive his plates of onion rings from our waitress. My omelet came soon after, along with a wilted stuffed pepper. I finished my eggs quickly and OWEN looked pleased when I ate some of his onion rings. The sight of me eating seemed to amuse him and he insisted I try some of his stuffed pepper before he would agree to help me examine Laury's borrowing history. As it turned out, the pepper was stuffed with a foul-tasting mixture of cabbage and caraway seeds. OWEN delighted in the unhappy faces I made as I chewed. There was some discussion as to whether the bite I had taken was big enough before I pushed the plates aside and placed the printout from the library between us.

"Fine," OWEN said, disappointed. "But if I find anything important in here, you have to eat more pepper."

"If you tell me anything useful about Sarah Laury, I'll finish the whole thing."

In a flash OWEN had removed his blazer and was rolling up his shirtsleeves.

"You're on."

The list was in chronological order and the items toward the top were the sort of books one would expect any bright young woman to borrow: *Jane Eyre, Madame Bovary, To the Lighthouse.* There were also books that had obviously been borrowed in response to a specific class or assignment: Campbell's *History of the French and Indian War, A Critical Companion to* The House of Seven Gables. It wasn't until halfway down the list that something caught my attention: *The Anatomy of a City* by Andre Denard.

"Oh, Denard!" I said to OWEN.

I only meant to tell him it was one of my favorite books, but OWEN assumed it was of importance and read a copy of it he found online. He nodded and said that a 1,500-page treatise on the infrastructure of modern cities seemed a little dense for an undergrad.

"Not really," I said. "I loved that book when I was her age."

"Yeah," he said. "And you're a giant weirdo."

I was about to go on defending the book when I noticed the next titles on the list. I recognized them immediately as the work of fringe sociologists: *Infrastructure and Institutionalized Oppression, Agents of Gentrification, Civil Revolutionaries, Radical Communities.* These were texts written by the sort of riffraff who hadn't been able to get into the National Engineering Academy and had studied anthropology at Brown while smoking marijuana and misquoting

Foucault to one another at parties. But perhaps the most troubling book on the list was the last item, which had been checked out two weeks before Laury's disappearance and had since accrued over $12.85 in late fees: *A Beginner's Guide to Esperanto*. OWEN whistled.

"Well, whatever Kirklin's got planned," he said, "I'm guessing she's into it."

I pulled out the bound issues of *The Marigold* and began flipping through them in search of Laury's contributions. Her monthly column was titled the Laury Perspective, a 1,200-word box in the upper-right-hand corner of the opinion page. The grainy black-and-white photo next to her byline showed her in a ponytail and a white polo. She looked like a normal college student, as opposed to the young celebrity whose face was usually reproduced on the heavy, glossy stock of popular magazines. The first few installments of the column were socially minded but restrained. I skimmed a few pieces on antibullying, the value of contributing one's time to a charitable organization, and a charming piece on dining etiquette:

> Though the American style of holding one's fork is of course perfectly acceptable, allow me to enumerate what I feel are several distinct advantages to the Continental style.

A month after Laury had checked out *The Anatomy of a City*, the topics she covered had grown edgier. She wrote a slightly provocative piece on commuter attrition, "Parking Meter Rates Should Be Raised for Good of the City," and soon she was penning heated accusations against her father's administration, accusing members of his staff of negligence and even fraud.

There had been some mention in the mainstream press of Laury's public criticisms of her father, but nothing that would have prepared me for the inflammatory statements she had published regularly in *The Marigold*. It seemed strange that her writing hadn't caused more of a stir. I wondered aloud whether there may have been a deliberate cover-up and OWEN cut me off.

"Henry, it's a column on local government in a college newspaper. I can't believe *we're* reading it."

I could see he had a point, but if anyone had paid attention to said college newspaper, they might have stumbled across a particularly interesting item in its Clubs and Activities section. That's where I found a picture of Terrence Kirklin surrounded by a group of young people under a handmade banner identifying them as Newton's Future Municipal Leaders. I recognized the club as one of Garrett's school outreach programs. He had made participation mandatory for all of his admins. The week he made the announcement, Kirklin had flown down to Suitland just to slam a few doors and scream at Garrett for trying to turn him into a goddamned babysitter.

He seemed happy enough in the photograph, sitting front and center with half a dozen Newton students huddled around him. I had never seen Kirklin smiling before and if it weren't for his eye patch I probably wouldn't have recognized him. Laury was standing next to Kirklin's chair, her hand resting on his shoulder. The article continued onto the next page, where there was a photograph of Kirklin with his arm around Laury at a pizza fund-raiser for the group. They were standing close, with Laury's head almost resting on Kirklin's chest. They had the contented look of newlyweds.

From there we moved on to Laury's play, titled *The Man in the Tower*. While the tone of her later columns had been rather acerbic, her play was a surprisingly reflective story about a young woman who is driven mad by her many suitors and ends up fleeing her small village to live in the wilderness. *I can no longer live with so many eyes fixed so maniacally in my direction,* she proclaims as she flees into a dense wood. After wandering for some time and delivering a few monologues on the value of solitude and self-determination, she encounters a strange man named Majstro who lives in an ancient stone tower. He explains that he is a wizard responsible for maintaining the order of the universe and performs a few miracles for her benefit, moving the stars around the night sky, teaching her the language of trees, etc. The girl tells him about her troubles—*I am loved by too many and have been robbed of all quiet*—and he invites her to take refuge in his tower, where they conduct a series of philosophical dialogues regarding the baseness and corruption of humankind. Their discussions grow in intensity and eventually result in declarations of love between the two. From the tower they see that her suitors have followed her into the woods and Majstro offers to place the girl among the stars, where he can look after her and protect her from the relentlessness of those who are pursuing her. She happily accepts the offer and is turned into a constellation in the shape of a circle. The girl's suitors then find the wizard's tower and demand to know whether or not he has seen her. Without saying a word the wizard self-immolates and another circle appears in the sky, creating a figure eight.

OWEN was still frowning down at the last page when I asked him what he thought of it.

"You mean artistically?" he said, scrunching up his nose. "It's a bunch of confessional, pseudosymbolic garbage."

His hours of watching classic cinema with Klaus had clearly made him a bit of a snob when it came to narrative art.

"The whole thing is just a bunch of melodramatic whining dressed up in the laziest way possible. The suitors represent her fame. The forest, her burgeoning womanhood and corresponding confusion. The wizard, Kirklin. His control over the universe, Kirklin's influence in Metropolis. And don't get me started on that tower. She should have saved that imagery for her honeymoon, am I right?"

OWEN did have a point in that the one-to-one correspondence of the play's various elements suggested it was the work of a literal thinker, with the exception of those stars forming a figure eight, which seemed uncharacteristically playful. Though if Majstro was Kirklin, and his control over the world represented his control over the city, it was possible that the end of the play meant he had hidden her somewhere in the city's infrastructure.

"That's good, Henry," OWEN said when I shared my theory. "So he hid her somewhere in the largest city in the country. We didn't need to read ninety pages of expressionist drivel to know that might be a possibility."

"Check the city's sewer system for any access tunnels shaped like figure eights."

"Nothing."

"What about the old subway lines?"

OWEN scratched his chin while he thought it over. "The old tracks were mostly straight lines running along avenues. And they were all abandoned twenty years before Kirklin came on as station chief. He only ever contributed algorithms for the current system."

OWEN saw my face brighten when he mentioned Kirklin's transit algorithms.

"No way," he said, looking down sadly at the uneaten pepper. "That's not possible."

I put some money on the table and gathered up the library materials so I could dump them into the trash on my way to the exit. I knew where we would find Sarah Laury.

"I said it's not possible," OWEN called out across the diner. "Someone would have noticed."

8 Most experts agree that when it comes to public transit in the twentieth century, the original subway system in Metropolis was among the worst in the world. Though, really it hadn't even been a system in the proper sense of the word. Each line was built and maintained separately by independent operators who had set out to provide service for specific parts of the city. The implementation of a comprehensive citywide transit system was deemed too expensive, and so for decades the city's subways were abandoned to the free market. Coverage was limited and required commuters to put up with circuitous travel routes; in order to get from Mark and Verdi in the South Side to Little India in the East Side, one would have to take the Express Intracity twenty minutes in the wrong direction, then walk to Murch to catch the Rapid East.

By 1961, there were over two hundred different train lines in the city, each with its own fare structure and unique token. A famous photo from the *Metropolis Examiner* shows commuters in raincoats standing in front of a subway entrance and sorting through handfuls of tokens to see if they have the right one for that particular line. In the mid-1960s the state legislature attempted to solve the issue by establishing the Metropolis Transit Authority, which began to buy up the old lines and manage them as a single public benefit corporation. But the individual lines were still so far apart and discontinuous that the MTA was unable to provide effective service.

The problem wasn't fully addressed until 1978 when Albert Tessman, our Metropolis station chief at the time, finally wrangled political support for a unified system, which ended up being the largest public transportation project in the nation's history. While some of the older tunnels and stations were repurposed, most were ultimately abandoned for the new network of concentric and interconnected hubs with parallel local and express tracks. The system also included an exterior loop of bullet trains that could carry riders from one end of the city to the other in a little over thirty minutes. When work was completed, average ridership increased from 60 million passengers a year to 4.2 billion, making it one of the most heavily utilized transit systems in the world.

There was no room for error, which was why Kirklin's contributions to the city's train schedule algorithms had been one of his most impressive accomplishments. Previous station chiefs had been happy to keep the system running at all, whereas Kirklin had been famous for his aggressive, "not good enough" approach. Within his first five years, he shaved a little over a minute off the average commute duration. Every year after that, if the duration failed to be reduced by at least five seconds, he would pressure city hall and Suitland alike until the MTA got more trains or better signals or more personnel or whatever he felt was lacking. The result was that after twenty years of his service, the movement of trains in Metropolis's subway system was seamless and unrelenting, a complex unison of stops and starts like the beating of a monstrous heart.

So it was no wonder that OWEN remained unconvinced of my hypothesis even as he flashed a fake transit pass at the bar code reader to get us into the J1 station at 97th Street. The idea of Kirklin trying to hide Laury somewhere in the city's active rail system was admittedly outlandish, but it was also perfectly in keeping with his audaciousness up to that point.

The station's narrow stairwell eventually opened up into one of Metropolis's cavernous subway stations, where the walls were massive slabs of coffered stone that rose up and converged overhead in clean, minimalist arches. Several auxiliary lines had been closed as a result of the previous day's attacks, so the station was especially busy. I picked up a subway map from a nearby kiosk and asked OWEN to pull the agency's records from our shared database with the MTA on any changes to train service that had been implemented by Kirklin within the last year.

"Done," he said. "No major changes. A few tweaks here and there. I'm telling you, Henry. These schedules are tight. The track usage is almost continuous."

"Almost?"

"Well, Kirklin decreased the number of stops on the R4 line, which shares some of its tracks with the A3 and C1 trains. That puts a three-minute gap between all three lines, which used to follow one another in two-minute intervals. But that's not significant—"

OWEN thought for a moment, then corrected himself.

"Except he also made changes to the Q7, which now runs

as a shuttle between 13th and 48th Streets. That lets all E trains circle around Ansit Square. And the R4 shares some track with the E5 once it's east of the park, which makes a five-minute gap."

He worked his way through Kirklin's changes, which began to run together. I tried to follow along on my subway map, but OWEN was going too fast.

"He did it," he said finally, his doubt giving way to astonishment. "He hid an entire train."

I held up the map between us.

"Show me."

OWEN projected a two-inch line of blue light onto the map. It started on the L1 line in the North Side and then curved down, switching to the M1 and crossing all the way down to Center City. The light continued moving southwest, parallel with the F3, before gradually curving east and back up to the North Side. The route formed, roughly, a figure eight.

According to OWEN, the circuit was uninterrupted except for two daily stops in the Lower West Side. For two minutes the train had to be redirected off the main tracks in midtunnel before continuing on its way.

"We're just in time for the first daily stop," OWEN said. "It'll be south of here on the F3 line in about twenty minutes."

Just then a downtown-bound train pulled into the station. I observed the crowds filling the platform, then winked at OWEN and nodded toward the tracks. He smiled, his eyes full of impish glee.

As we ran toward the train, OWEN turned us into

blood-splattered surgeons. He was holding a Styrofoam cooler out in front of him.

"Everybody out of our way," he shouted. "We've got a human brain here and it's not getting any fresher."

"A brain?" a young man on the platform called out as other passengers stepped off the train to make room for us.

"That's right," OWEN said. "We have to get this thing downtown and put it in some sick kid."

It was absurd, but I knew firsthand what it was like to have OWEN's confidence throw you. On the train, a young woman even offered him her seat, which, graciously, he refused.

○——○

We got off at 26th Street and climbed down onto the tracks once the train left the station. OWEN timed our run so we were able to slip into a maintenance shaft just as an express train shot through the tunnel at full speed. From there we moved forward in twenty-second bursts, stopping to take shelter between the exposed steel columns in the center of the tunnel that separated the two sets of tracks. There wasn't much space between the trains and I had to press myself against each column to keep from being hit.

Eventually we reached an area where the tunnel grew wider with a third set of tracks that stretched a few hundred yards along the first two. I was still trying to catch my breath when I heard a train rumbling slowly up the tunnel. There was a metallic clink and the arriving train rolled onto the turnoff before coming to a stop with a hard blast of its air brakes. It was a heavy locomotive pulling ten weld cars, the sort of reinforced and stripped-down commuter cars that were used to transport equipment or new sections of rail. It occurred to me that perhaps all OWEN and I had succeeded in doing was finding a supply train that no one had bothered recording in the MTA database. But OWEN looked excited and, after one more express train shot past, he waved me out onto the tracks and we both ran in a half crouch toward the rear of the train.

We climbed up onto the back of the last car and stood on either side of its sliding door. I leaned in to peek through its small window, but it had been covered from the inside with dark cloth. OWEN disappeared as the train began to pull back onto the express tracks.

"I'll keep out of sight," he said in my ear. "We might need the element of surprise if we run into any of Kirklin's people."

I nodded and pulled hard on the door. As I stepped into the unlit car, OWEN shined a light from the tie clip. The interior was empty except for something hanging on the far wall next to the other door. I made my way up the car and saw that it was a blue plaid raincoat hanging on a metal hook. On the floor next to it was a matching pair of rain boots resting on a welcome mat embroidered with a white horse jumping over a brush fence.

Sarah Laury was here.

"You have forty minutes until the next stop," OWEN said. "Find her before then so we can get her off the train. I'll lead you through the tunnels from there."

I gave the tie clip a thumbs-up, but when I looked down I

saw that my hands and my shirt were stained with rust from hugging all those columns.

"OWEN," I said, "do you think you could clean me up a little bit?"

"Good idea," he said. "It's not every day you get to reverse kidnap a celebrity. You'll want to look your best."

Within seconds I was wearing a fresh suit and my hands looked clean. As for the smell of sweat and booze, I had to rely on faith alone she wouldn't notice.

I entered the next car and was surprised to find myself standing in a tastefully decorated kitchen with dark granite countertops and matching stainless steel appliances. Overhead, large PA speakers filled the car with classical music.

"What is this?" I said.

"Mozart's Third Violin Concerto," OWEN said. "G major."

When I clarified that I was talking about the kitchen I could feel OWEN shrug.

"Joke's on us," he said. "I guess the train wasn't even the crazy part."

A mesh bag of red and yellow bell peppers swung on a silver hook under the cherrywood cabinets, while fresh pears and apples rested in a bowl fixed permanently to the countertop. On the walls were several art prints of stylized kitchen utensils done in bold, warm colors. Except for an empty cereal bowl and spoon in the large double sink, the room could have been a photograph out of *Metropolis Living*. Subway cars in Metropolis were designed five feet wider than in most cities in order to accommodate the high number of commuters, and so this kitchen was even larger than the ones I would have found in a luxury condo in Center City. The only thing that broke the illusion was the gentle movement of the car from side to side.

In the next car I passed through a full dining room with a drum chandelier that swung in a slow circle over a long oak table. There was a single place setting next to a large white button built into the tabletop. When I pressed it the plate and silverware began to slide about the table. When I pushed it again, they came to a stop.

"Look at this," I said to OWEN. "Must be magnetized."

"That's great," he said, his voice beginning to crackle from the electromagnetic interference. "But are we down here looking for Sarah Laury or for a table with a big magnet in it?"

I moved quickly through the next car, a bedroom that was empty except for a walk-in closet that ran the length of the car and a white canopy bed. Next was a library, its wooden shelves built into the side of the car at a slant to keep the books in place. Between two such shelves was a Louis XV–style writing desk and an equally ornate padded chair pulled away from it at an angle. On the wall hung a lithograph of a young woman standing in the back of a carriage surrounded by soldiers. She held out her right hand to the men in exhortation and lightly gripped a spear with her left. The caption read *Boadicea Haranguing the Britons*. Near the desk was a light metal waste bin bolted into the floor. It was filled with torn and crumpled pieces of paper. I retrieved a sheet and opened it, holding it up to the light. It was covered in Esperanto in a neat, cursive hand.

"OWEN," I said. "Can I get a translation?"

He cleared his throat and began, "The importance of disrupting the continuum of western culture is self-evident when one considers the fact that—"

Several words were crossed out before beginning again.

"The necessity of disrupting the continuum of western culture—As it stands, the continuum of western culture—Western culture, when considered as a continuum—The reason we have decided to disrupt the continuum of western culture—"

From there the text was scratched out and OWEN's voice trailed off. There was a moment of silence as he and I contemplated the disturbing content of those fragments that I eventually broke by offering up a slightly dismayed, "Yikes."

"Wait," OWEN said. "Listen to this."

Farther down the page Laury had included a quote from an article written by Kirklin for the *Journal of Auxiliary Languages*. OWEN translated it as follows:

> *Because organic languages are a vessel for cultural information, one of the great advantages of a constructed language is its cultural emptiness, allowing speakers to step outside of many pernicious social constructs and thus communicate with a higher degree of freedom . . . Racism and classism in the United States are power relationships that are perpetually reinforced by the English language. Without the benefit of English, both could be extinguished within a few generations.*

chair and thrown to the ground. There was a foot on my chest and through a dark haze I saw a man in a black suit point the nozzle of a fire extinguisher in the direction of the crates. As I lost consciousness I heard a long blast of CO_2, followed by the men around me shouting, "It's out! It's out!"

12 I woke up coughing and found myself once again tied to a chair. Someone said something in Esperanto. The room was bright and I was surrounded by unfamiliar shapes. I had to squint to make out that I was in a small, virtually featureless room with a cement floor and walls of unpainted cinder block. One of Kirklin's agents tried a few more questions in Esperanto before addressing me in English.

"Are you awake? Can you understand me?"

I probably looked like I was about to say something until I threw up in my lap.

The man took a step back and began discussing something with another agent.

I rested my eyes and eventually heard a door open, followed by Kirklin's voice.

"Henry?"

I opened one eye and nodded, feeling that same painful fullness in my head.

Kirklin looked back over his shoulder at the agents, who were still standing at attention, and spoke to them in English for my benefit.

"How am I supposed to talk to him if he's half-dead?"

"None of us touched him," one of the men said. "He seems to have done this to himself."

Kirklin looked back to me. He took me in for a moment before shaking his head, then pulled a chair from the other side of the room and sat across from me.

"It was you at Clairmont?"

I nodded again.

Kirklin looked up to the ceiling. It was clear he was doing his best to hold back a massive welling up of rage. But there was also a strange gleam in his eye, as if the whole thing secretly pleased him. Eventually he let out a sigh and smiled sadly before leaning in close.

"You wanted to protect Metropolis so you leveled half a city block?"

"Yes."

He ran a finger along the shoulder of my jacket, examining the dust on his fingertip.

"You're a fine young man," he said, softly. "You should have been one of mine."

He stood up.

"No torture this time, Henry. You've earned a fast death."

He spoke to his men in English again so I would understand. "Take him out to the platform. She wants to do it in front of the muster."

As Kirklin left, two men approached me, tilting my chair back and carrying me out the door. I heard the noise of a distant crowd grow steadily louder. At first I saw only high ceilings with exposed rafters, but as that noise grew closer, I saw men and women in black suits all around me, cold faces looking down in disapproval. The room was dark except for a perimeter of bright lights at the edge of the crowd. I was taken up onto a raised platform that was otherwise empty.

The crowd went quiet and I was left to sit there in silence with hundreds of Kirklin's agents observing me.

I turned my head to avoid the blare of the lights and saw a stockpile of countless weapons arranged neatly in open crates. No one in the crowd seemed to be armed, but agents with clipboards were walking through the stacks of crates and making notes, conferring with one another and pointing toward the crowd as if discussing how best to disseminate those deadly wares.

Even this activity stopped when from the other side of the room came the sound of confident footsteps. There was an air of expectation and reverence. I turned to see Sarah Laury climb a rise of steps and join me up on the platform. She was wearing the same red dress from the night before, but with a green canvas army coat over it, the large sleeves rolled up over her delicate wrists. She was holding a rifle and her face was painted like a skull.

She stood over me, looking down with a purity in her gaze that made her seem both there and not there. A look of cosmic judgment. She turned to face the gathered crowd and addressed them in a powerful voice. "Saluton, miaj kolegoj."

She launched into a spirited oration, in which I supposed she was railing against the continuum of western culture. Without understanding a word, I could sense that she was filling that large space with a brilliant anger. It was also clear from the rigid attentiveness of the crowd that they wanted nothing more than to bring about by any means necessary the world of which she spoke. Even Kirklin was staring up at her in wonder from the front of the crowd.

I tried to see if I could ruin her speech by throwing up

again, but couldn't make it happen. Breathing was an effort and the sad thought occurred to me that the only act of defiance still open to me would be to die before she had the chance to shoot me.

Laury turned from the audience and addressed a few words to me in Esperanto. It was some booming, final condemnation and it sounded as if she expected a response. I pretended to give it some thought before responding with the only Esperanto I could recall from that morning, "Mi devas pisi."

She was unperturbed by my answer and took a step back, pointing the barrel of her rifle at my chest.

I should say something, I thought. I wanted to say something real. Something without anger. Tell them why it was so important that they be stopped.

"Wait," I said. "Wait."

She made no motion to lower the rifle, but before I could ask her again, I heard my own disembodied voice, amplified, echoing throughout the room.

"Kirklin's men are just a bunch of stupid townie goons."

My face was suddenly projected forty feet high onto the wall to the right of the platform.

"And Kir—Ki—Excuse me," my face said. "Kirklin is a big grumpy weirdo. If we see him tomorrow, I'm going to tell him that to his face."

"You should," I heard OWEN's voice say off camera.

"I *will*," my face said.

My captors and I were watching footage of OWEN and me back in the Museum of History, drunk. While I had no idea how this was possible, I knew enough to dread what was coming next. My rant against Kirklin was even more insane and sexually depraved than I had remembered. I could scarcely follow the logic of it. One moment the Kirklin of my imagination was French-kissing an ostrich and the next he was working up the courage to press his butt up into the Liberty Bell.

I wondered if Kirklin's virus had allowed him to hack into OWEN's memory banks and if he was now showing this video as a kind of accusation. But when I looked down at Kirklin, he seemed taken aback. Sarah Laury too was staring up at my image in stunned, rifle-drooped confusion.

The silence of the crowd soon gave way to angry shouts and Kirklin began to issue orders to the agents in his vicinity, some of whom began to rush about in small groups looking for the source of the projection.

To the remaining crowd Sarah Laury called out something in Esperanto and pointed her rifle back at me. Before she could take the shot, the recording of me ended and another loud voice echoed throughout the crowd, "FBI. NOBODY MOVE."

As FBI agents in SWAT gear appeared all around the room, the surprised roar of Kirklin's agents was drowned out by a booming arrangement of the theme music from *The Magnificent Seven*. One agent popped up behind Laury and disarmed her. Others blocked the exit and secured the arsenal. The rest of the agents were soon joined by a large National Guard unit equipped for crowd control and, after some scattered fighting, Kirklin's people were subdued.

Laury attempted to run to Kirklin when he was discovered among the crowd and taken into custody, but was held back by two guardsmen, who were startled by her screams. Kirklin looked up at her with sadness and love as the FBI agents put his hands in restraints. He shouted something to her, but it was drowned out by her cries as well as the boisterous, triumphant music that had continued to swell from every direction. She kicked and bit at the guardsmen who were holding her back with such ferocity that several more men had to be called up to the platform in order to remove her from the building.

The FBI began escorting prisoners out of the building ten and twenty at a time. Kirklin was at the head of the first line and his men began to scream what sounded like encouragements to him in Esperanto while he was marched out.

As the mass arrests continued, OWEN appeared across from me on the platform. He chuckled at the sight of me tied to another office chair.

"Who would have thought," he said, lowering the volume of his own soundtrack so I could hear him. "Sarah Laury is one hell of a public speaker."

There was a drink in his hand.

"What is it with bloodthirsty megalomaniacs and public speaking?" he said, sitting next to me in a chair that he pulled from nowhere. "Humans are weird."

Then he asked, "Is it true what she said in her speech? Did you blow up the arsenal on Clairmont?"

I nodded and OWEN immediately burst out laughing.

"Nice job, dummy," he said. "Like twenty firemen died trying to put out that fire."

I slumped forward in my chair. I felt the life going out of me.

"Is that true?"

"No," OWEN said. "But it could have been. I mean, a munitions fire? Are you out of your mind?"

He pointed to a column of Kirklin's men being marched out of the warehouse with their hands bound.

"You see all this?" he said. "I helped the FBI track down Kirklin's arms dealer and he gave us a couple of addresses. Our response was all very tactical, very clever, very unlike a raging munitions fire within city limits. So—"

It was worth wondering how OWEN had managed to escape and strike up a working relationship with the FBI, but my body was failing and all I wanted was for OWEN to stop talking.

"So, what?" I said.

"So don't ditch me next time. I'm your friend and I'm better at this than you are."

Nearby, one of Kirklin's agents slipped out of his restraints and tried to take a swing at an FBI agent, but was quickly brought down by several guardsmen with stun sticks. OWEN watched the proceedings somewhat wistfully and said, "We could have made this happen together."

"OWEN," I said, "I think I'm dying."

He looked at me, confused for a moment, and then snapped his fingers. "Oh, that's right. I have my patch switched on in case I found you in a bad way. Let me turn it off and get a look at you."

"I'd stay seated."

OWEN almost flickered out when he saw the shape I was in. But instead of fainting, he told me to hold tight and stormed off into the crowd. Within a few minutes FBI agents were untying me and an air ambulance was called. A woman in FBI SWAT gear pulled OWEN's tie clip from the strap of her helmet and placed it in my hand while we waited for the EMTs.

"Keep him out of trouble," she said.

I don't remember being loaded into the helicopter, but I must have held on to the tie clip because OWEN was with me the whole time, kneeling next to the stretcher with his hand projected onto mine as the EMTs grew more and more concerned over my vitals, my unsteady breath fogging my oxygen mask.

It was nighttime and as we banked gently to the left I saw the bright lights of Center City shining below. OWEN followed my eyes and we stared out at the city together. It hurt to talk, but by slipping the tie clip under the mask I was able to make myself understood over the pounding of the rotors.

"What was that?" OWEN asked without taking his eyes off Metropolis.

"I said pour yourself a drink."

He laughed and then did so.

13 As I was admitted to the ICU at Metropolis Medical Center, OWEN slipped in amid the confusion and disguised himself as a doctor. Based on his knowledge that I had been involved in an explosion and whatever information he had been able to gather from the scan of my person he conducted on the flight over, he felt comfortable having the ICU staff start treatment for a condition he referred to as blast lung. He also told them to look for any internal bleeding or tertiary wounds. You can imagine my horror as I looked up in my semiconscious state and saw OWEN standing over me in a lab coat, shouting out orders to every health care professional in sight.

Later my actual doctor seemed confused as to who had initiated the majority of my treatments, but she admitted that the speedy diagnosis had probably saved my life. OWEN was sitting behind her in the corner of my hospital room, working on a crossword puzzle of his own devising. At the mention of saving my life, he continued to work on his puzzle and waved his hand dismissively in my direction as if to say, "Don't mention it."

She went on to inform me that I had a fracture in my left knee that would require extensive physical therapy. Even with a lot of hard work I would probably be walking with a cane for some time. As soon as she left, OWEN leapt up from his seat and began walking back and forth, experimenting with various styles of walking sticks.

"A cane?" he said. "You lucky son of a bitch."

OWEN had never used foul language in my company before, but after being embedded with an FBI SWAT team he was now swearing fairly regularly.

In his hand appeared a beech wood walking stick with a chrome eagle head for a handle. A brass jaguar on a shaft of blue ash. He cycled through diamond knob handles and gold lion heads. Shafts of walnut and padauk. Canes with swords in them and knotted shillelaghs.

"I'm going to get one too," he said. "Though, we can't both walk around with canes. We'd look like assholes. We can divide up the week. I'll take Monday, Wednesday, Friday and we'll alternate on weekends."

He twirled a cane whose handle featured a large pewter mermaid.

This was another in a series of remarks OWEN had made that suggested he anticipated working closely alongside me once we returned to Suitland. I had deflected these comments until now and I thought it would be best to address this most recent one at face value.

"I'll actually need a cane. You won't."

OWEN looked down at me from the foot of the bed and clutched his cane to his chest. "That's a horrible thing to say to somebody."

I was admitted for three weeks and OWEN seemed to enjoy our time in the hospital, ordering me a set of clothes online for my journey home, projecting old movies onto the wall of my room, and occasionally offering to order me pizzas or put in a good word for me with some of the attractive young women on the hospital staff.

I'd been avoiding what I assumed would be an awkward conversation, and so it wasn't until our plane ride back to Suitland that I asked OWEN how he had managed to escape and collaborate with the FBI. He seemed surprised that I mentioned his confinement to the tower so casually and I knew he was expecting an apology. But he had too much pride in his ingenuity to keep the story to himself.

Using his own database, OWEN had made a series of late-night calls to higher-ups at the Port Authority, pretending to be someone from the governor's office. It took several tries before he found someone who could send a maintenance worker to recover what he described over the phone as an important piece of monitoring equipment. OWEN gave detailed instructions as to where he was to be found and the maintenance worker recovered him within the hour. Unfortunately, his rescuer was apparently annoyed at having been called in so late over something so seemingly unimportant. Instead of dropping the tie clip off at the nearest police station as OWEN had ordered over the phone, the man called his supervisor and reported that he hadn't found anything. He then chucked the tie clip from the driver's-side window of his van on his way home.

The clip landed in an alley, where it was eventually discovered by a seventy-year-old woman named Malvina who had come outside to give her leftovers to the stray cats who lived around her building's dumpster. OWEN impressed her with a few illusions, then convinced her to take him to the police in exchange for three wishes. She asked for a washing machine and a dryer. When OWEN asked her what her third wish was, she said she wanted the washer and dryer to be new.

"Don't worry," OWEN interrupted his story to add. "I've already made the arrangements and the agency has sent her the best washer and dryer on the market. I also sent her a few thousand dollars just to be nice."

"How many is a few?"

OWEN shrugged and resumed his story, which now had him arriving at a quiet police station in the East Side, where he pretended to be an automated message caught on a loop, identifying the clip as property of the FBI and demanding that it be returned to the Metropolis field office immediately. According to the officers on duty at the Seventy-Third Precinct, "immediately" meant 10:00 A.M. the next day. Once he reached the FBI, he managed to convince everyone there that he was special tech on loan from FBI headquarters in Washington. Combining what he knew about Kirklin's operation with FBI resources, OWEN had been able to find Kirklin's arms dealer in a matter of minutes. He was a nineteen-year-old boy named Anthony Boxler who lived in the basement of his parents' split-level in a nearby suburb. Widely known on anarchist message boards all over the Deep Web as proxy_moxy, the boy had brokered the sale of millions of dollars' worth of weapons online and coordinated with Kirklin's agents embedded throughout Metropolis's maritime freight infrastructure to sneak two cargo vessels loaded with arms into the city. Boxler told the FBI everything he knew and from there it was only a matter of organizing the raids with the National Guard on Kirklin's remaining facilities. By the time they were ready, I had already blown up the building on Clairmont and the only people left in the Wilmington Avenue high-rise were the agents who were piloting drones over what were believed to be Kirklin's next intended targets. On the way to Kirklin's third and final base, a refurbished marine construction facility along the Lawrence River, OWEN confided in a Special Agent Boyle, the person in charge of leading the raids, that after Kirklin was apprehended the tie clip needed to be returned to a Henry Thompson at the USMS.

"I didn't expect us to run into you there," he said. "So you can't say you risked your life for nothing. Agent Boyle's time is valuable and you saved her a trip to the post office."

I had come to understand that OWEN's needling was his way of expressing a certain kind of affection. I had a large cast on my left leg and from the expression of discomfort on my face in the cabin of that small agency plane, he had most likely decided that the moment called for a bit of good-natured ribbing. I suppose I was relieved that OWEN was in high spirits as we returned to Suitland even though I was sure he had to know that it would be the end of our working together. After all, as long as OWEN existed in his present form, at least one aspect of Kirklin's plan was still at work. His virus.

Garrett had kept my presence in Metropolis under wraps, so OWEN and I were welcomed back to headquarters quietly. We met with Garrett and Klaus in a secure meeting room in the admin sector in order to debrief them without fear of being overheard by any of our colleagues or, worse, the oversight committee members who were still lingering around the agency in search of improprieties.

I was slow entering the room, still awkward on my crutches. OWEN marched in ahead of me, airily embracing Klaus, both of them laughing and exchanging pleasantries in German. Garrett placed a hand on my shoulder and said he was glad to have me back.

I thanked him and remained standing while the three of them sat around the room's small conference table. I told Klaus that his new interface had unlimited potential and that OWEN had single-handedly saved Metropolis. Here OWEN raised a finger to signal an interruption and announced to the room, "I also kept his tie straight."

I told OWEN to give Garrett and Klaus access to our memory partition and encouraged both of them to go through OWEN's memory banks. I then put the clip on the table and told them what else they would see if they watched the footage, explaining that while the end result had been desirable, OWEN's current configuration was erratic and still contaminated by Kirklin's virus. I told them that OWEN himself had admitted the only way to remedy this was a complete memory wipe and a reinstallation of the interface.

I didn't have much to add to that recommendation, so I thanked them for their time and excused myself.

Given OWEN's powers of display, I had been expecting a scene. But as I left the room, he was looking down at the table without saying a word.

If he'd asked me why I did it, I would have told him that I'd already had my world disappear once, when the Lake Shore Limited left the tracks. I wasn't going to put the first home I'd known since then at risk by keeping around a vestige of Kirklin's madness.

I told myself that OWEN's friendship had been nothing but an illusion, a quirk of damaged software.

I walked back to my office, which was exactly as I'd left it. There was a stuffiness in the air that had probably always been there but that I'd never been away long enough to notice. I lowered myself into my chair and adjusted the model train on my desk before sorting through the file folders and papers I'd left in neat stacks. In Metropolis, I had been frightened and out of my depth. But here everything seemed so much less complicated. The reassuring orderliness of this place I had long since learned to call home was already welcoming me back and I suffered no doubt that I had done the right thing with regard to OWEN. I was in my element.

○———○

With Kirklin in custody and the agency's woes all attributable to him, the oversight committee eventually withdrew their request for Garrett's resignation. Soon the agency was back to normal and I was in the field doing what I loved. Right away I went out to South Bend to renovate the city's central bus station. When the work was finished, I stood leaning on my cane in the station's empty lobby and admired where the scuffed drywall had been replaced with handsome stone tile and where the water-damaged ceilings had been ripped out. Now there were high windows flooding the place with sunlight, endowing the very idea of bus travel with an air of nostalgic adventure.

But even though it only took one glance to know that

South Bend's new bus station was perfect, I still felt that something was missing, like some aspect of my earlier happiness at the agency hadn't come back with me from Metropolis. That day in Indiana I imagined OWEN standing next to me in the station, taking in all my hard work. I was surprised when my own vision of him turned to me and said sharply, "Henry, is this how you're spending your time?"

That night, I took my team to a sports bar to celebrate a successful end to the project. Garrett had given me a wealth of new responsibilities and I now had a host of deferential young agents at my disposal. I was sitting at a table with a handful of them when across the room I noticed Helen Roth, the economist who had participated in my capture in the abandoned transit tunnels of Metropolis.

Now she was sitting at a bar in Indiana nursing a nearly empty glass of beer. She'd chopped off her long braid and was wearing a cropped blond wig. She caught me staring and we locked eyes for a moment. As soon as she recognized me her face took on a desperate, hunted look. My first few weeks back in Suitland I had been worried that the agency might be targeted for retribution by one of Kirklin's loose agents, but her reaction told me Kirklin's people were all too busy trying to stay ahead of the FBI to be dangerous.

As the bar grew crowded with locals, she kept her eyes on me, waiting to see what I was going to do. I excused myself from the table and headed toward the bar, where I ordered a drink for myself and asked the bartender to send another round to Roth along with a napkin on which I wrote, "Truce."

I returned to my table slowly, still leaning heavily on my

cane. When I finally took my seat and looked back in her direction, I saw a full beer in front of her seat and a crumpled napkin. She was gone.

At the table my agents talked among themselves over the noise of the bar while I sipped a glass of Scotch and watched a muted television on the wall that was turned to the news. They were still running stories on the attacks whenever they could, so I wasn't surprised when I saw a picture of Kirklin's face next to the quote, "I will be at war with our government as long as the government is at war with its own poor and disenfranchised citizens." Soon after, the bartender found me and handed me a folded napkin. Inside Roth had written, "Iru al infero."

I had already forgotten what little Esperanto I had learned in Metropolis, so I took out my new agency phone and read the phrase into it. OWEN's old animation popped up and announced proudly, "Esperanto: Go to hell." His artificial intelligence had all been stripped down, so it must have been my imagination that OWEN looked a little pleased with Roth's message.

Garrett had taken my recommendation to have Klaus delete OWEN's infected interface. But instead of rebooting it and rolling it out agency-wide, Klaus had opted instead to stick with the old OWEN-linked smartphones for the time being. Most of the other agents were still using their own privately purchased cell phones, but I found myself drawn to the old OWEN interface.

Garrett confided that Klaus had been devastated by the order to delete the latest iteration of OWEN's interface, since the process of socializing it had been such a lengthy and personal one. I suppose I knew how Klaus felt. I missed OWEN on nights like this, when I was doing my best to be sociable with my subordinates. Getting drinks after the completion of a project had been a custom I'd initiated and was, I knew, contrary to my reputation at the agency. For the first ten minutes or so, the agents in my command would ask me polite questions related to our assignment and we might even manage some general small talk about the town in which we found ourselves. But I still didn't know anyone with whom it would have been appropriate or even desirable to spend an entire night drinking and talking. Hell, I would have liked to talk to Roth for a while. Forgetting everything that had happened in Metropolis, it would have been nice to spend an evening with a peer who was passionate about the world she lived in. Staring down at her note, all I could think was that I wasn't aware of anyone on earth who was, for whatever reason, truly excited to know me.

The only person who'd ever come close I'd betrayed. I told myself I'd done it because it was the right thing to do, but part of me suspected I'd just been worried that, if OWEN stuck around, his social and emotional intelligence would have eventually developed to the point where he would have understood that I wasn't a person worth knowing. I had long before made the calculation in my most private self that there was less risk in relying on predetermined guidelines than in trying to blunder my way toward the mystery of people's love.

It was my understanding that OWEN's old interface had been kept active for a while in some limited capacity so Klaus could conduct a host of final tests. He had only been shut down a few days before that night. Klaus had invited me, at

OWEN's request, to attend a small good-bye ceremony. Apparently they planned to watch *The Magnificent Seven* and have a few drinks. I was already in Indiana, so I declined.

I caught one of my agents looking at me with concern and realized I had been staring off. I excused myself and left an expense card with one of them, telling them to enjoy themselves while keeping in mind we all had an early flight.

At the hotel, I raided the minibar. Watching C-SPAN in a drunken haze, I found the napkin with Roth's message in my pants pocket and, without knowing what I was doing, took out a pen and added beneath it what I could remember from Kirklin's quote that I had seen on the news. I looked at my handwriting, meditating on Kirklin's fall. My mind began making loose connections that I couldn't quite follow and I told myself that if I could just figure out what had driven such a brilliant man with so many laudable ideals to commit such horrible acts, then I would be able to understand why it had been necessary to delete his virus and in doing so destroy OWEN.

The next morning I woke with a headache and found that I had laid the napkin carefully on top of my travel bag. I examined it for a while in the faint early-morning light coming through the curtains, wondering what I had meant by it.

○———○

Back at headquarters later that morning, I cleared my schedule and ran a report. I found every project proposal I had ever submitted to Garrett and looked at which had been approved, which had been rejected, and the per capita income for the cities attached to each proposal.

In my twelve years at the agency, I had submitted over 430 project proposals with an approval rate of 55 percent, just above average for someone in the field. When I compared the approvals and rejections to the per capita income for each target city, there was a positive correlation of 73 percent, meaning the wealthier the city was, the more likely it was to have a project approved. After spending the rest of the morning correcting the data to include the per capita income of the specific areas within each city that would have been affected by my proposals, there was a positive correlation of 98 percent.

With my new responsibilities, I now had access to the agency's administrative records. I was able to pull up most of the paperwork associated with my proposals, including the review notes that Garrett and his staff had circulated among themselves during the evaluation process. I didn't have to look long before I started to see references like this one: "Area currently subject to freezing in accordance with the mayor's office." Elsewhere I saw that dozens of my proposals had been rejected with the entire review document containing the single word: "Freezing."

I put together a comprehensive report and scheduled a meeting with Garrett. He looked it over at his desk while I sat across from him. After a few minutes, he nodded and placed the report to one side. He rubbed his eyes before crossing his legs and leaning back in his chair.

"This all seems pretty straightforward," he said. "What's your question?"

"I want you to tell me what freezing is," I said.

"You've been here a long time now. You know what it is."

"No, sir, I don't think I do."

He smiled quizzically at me for a moment, trying to decide whether I was joking or not. When I made no indication that I was, he continued in a tone that suggested he was surprised at the question but more than happy to answer it.

"When you start working on a project you don't just go to a city and start making unilateral changes, do you?"

"No, sir."

"Exactly, you build relationships with the city council, the mayor's office, et cetera. If the head of a city's DOT doesn't trust you, you're going to have a hell of a time getting them to let you do a thorough audit of their bus system. My office has to maintain the same sort of relationships and my staff takes those relationships into account when we're considering projects for approval."

"What I'm wondering, sir, is why any of what you just described would amount to us not offering our services to the places that need them the most."

Garrett raised his eyebrows and then laughed as if he couldn't believe that I of all people was wasting his time with this.

"Okay," he said, rubbing his eyes for a moment as if to gather his thoughts. "Let's say there's a city with an economically depressed neighborhood. Poor people live there, because they can afford to live there and they can afford to live there because it's less desirable. Who knows. It just is. Could be the school system, lack of commercial diversity, inadequate transportation, untended infrastructure. You and I

EXCELLENT BASS FILLET RECIPE

4	bass fillets	2	T. parsley, chopped
2	T. butter	I	lemon for juice
I	green pepper, sliced	I	potato, sliced
I	onion, sliced		salt and pepper

Spray a large piece of aluminum foil with nonstick spray or brush with vegetable oil. Lay potato slices on the foil the length of fillets. Lay slices of onion on the potato slices, then lay the fillets on the onion slices. Sprinkle with salt and pepper as desired, and add the chopped parsley and lemon juice. Lay a couple slices of green pepper next and then a layer of potato slices and spread with butter. Wrap and enclose with aluminum foil. Cook on an outdoor grill for 15 minutes on each side. The time could vary a little depending on your heat.

Don Kissaw
Urbana, IL

Don Kissaw

BROILED BASS WITH LEMON BUTTER

1½ lbs. bass fillets	snipped parsley
2 T. butter melted	lemon wedges
2 T. lemon juice	

SHORE LUNCH

EASY MEAL

Place the fish in a single layer on a greased rack of an unheated broiler pan. Tuck under and trim the edges. Combine with butter and lemon juice. Garnish with parsley and lemon wedges.

Linda Rosencrans
Warsaw, IN

RUSTY'S BUTTERED BASS

2–4 lbs. bass fillets	1–2 sticks of butter
1 large onion, chopped	salt and pepper
1–2 green bell peppers, chopped	garlic powder
	lemon pepper
2–3 slices bacon, cut into small pieces	

In a cast iron pan, melt ½ stick of butter. Cook onion, green peppers and bacon until soft. Add bass fillets, seasonings and more butter. Cook, stirring frequently, on medium heat until the bass mixes well with the other ingredients. Salt and pepper to taste.

Rusty Robbins
Saint Johns, PA

ORIENTAL SMALLMOUTH

1 lb. smallmouth bass, cleaned, boned and cut into ¼-inch strips	8 T. white vinegar
	8 T. sugar
1 pkg. ramen noodles	1 8-oz. pkg. fresh bean sprouts
½ cup vegetable oil	
4 eggs	1 8-oz. pkg. ground peanuts
1 8-oz. pkg. tofu, cut into ½-inch cubes	
	2 green onions, finely sliced
8 T. soy sauce	8 lime slices

Cook the ramen noodles by boiling for three minutes and adding flavor pack. Then heat a large skillet and add vegetable oil. When it's hot, reduce the heat to medium and cook smallmouth bass until done. Remove the bass from the oil and cook 4 eggs. Quickly stir and add tofu and stir fry for 3 minutes. Add noodles and bass; reduce the heat and simmer for 10 minutes. Now add the soy sauce, vinegar and sugar. Turn up the heat to high and toss well. Stir in bean sprouts and peanuts and remove from heat and serve. Garnish with green onion and lime wedges.

Bruce Haacker
So. Elgin, IL

Bruce Haacker

BUTTERMILK CATFISH

4	large catfish fillets (about 2 lbs.)	1	cup buttermilk
1	large yellow onion, thinly sliced	1	large lemon, quartered
2	cloves garlic, peeled and finely chopped	2	T. olive oil favorite seasoning, to taste

Clean catfish fillets and dry them with paper towels. Then place the catfish into a large glass baking dish so the fish is on a single level. Cover with the buttermilk. You may have to use more of the buttermilk than the one cup; this is ok. Let marinate for at least one hour; longer is fine, but not more than two hours.

After one hour, remove the fish and gently blot excess buttermilk. In a large nonstick frypan, heat the olive oil on high and add garlic and onions. While the onions are cooking, salt and pepper the fish, gently pressing the seasoning into the flesh on both sides. Once the onions are cooked until they are clear, place the fillets on top of the onions and cook on each side for about 5 minutes. Turn down the heat to simmer and cover the pan for an additional 5 to 7 minutes, depending on the thickness of the fillet. If you enjoy your fish moist, remove and serve. For dryer fish, take the cover off and cook for an additional 5 minutes.

To serve, place fillet on a plate, place some of the onions and garlic on top of the fish and squeeze the juice of a quarter lemon on top. Serve with butter, herb rice and a very nice California Chardonnay or white zinfandel wine.

Warren Heinemann
Livermore, CA

CATFISH APPETIZERS

2 lbs. catfish fillets	1 cup sour cream
1 cup cheese crackers, finely crushed	1/4 cup bleu cheese, crumbled
1/2 cup Parmesan cheese, grated	1/2 cup onion, finely chopped
1/2 cup butter or margarine, melted	1/4 tsp. salt
1/4 cup sesame seeds	parsley, chopped
	salt and pepper

To make the dip, combine the sour cream, bleu cheese, onion and salt. Garnish with chopped parsley. Refrigerate while the fish is cooking. Preheat the oven to 400°. Salt and pepper fillets, then cut them into 1-inch cubes. Mix the cracker crumbs, Parmesan cheese and sesame seeds. Dip the catfish cubes in the melted margarine, then roll in cracker crumb mixture and place them about 1/2 inch apart on well greased (or foil lined) baking sheets. Bake for 20 minutes or until fish is golden brown. Serve with dip. Makes about 6 dozen appetizers.

John Anthony Kostick
Sylmar, CA

TEXAS GOLDEN CATFISH NUGGETS

	catfish (½ inch thick), crappie or other fish	2	tsp. pepper
2	lb. bag (5½ cups) ground corn meal	1½	T. cayenne pepper
2	T. salt	1	T. garlic powder
			lemon pepper

First cut the catfish into nuggets 1½ inch thick. Mix corn meal, salt, pepper and cayenne pepper in a half-gallon freezer bag. The fish needs to be damp but not real wet. Shake the lemon pepper on the fish. Place only enough of the meal mix into the freezer bag for the amount of fish you are going to cook and shake to coat (remaining meal mix keeps well in freezer). Put the meal-coated fish on a plate or cookie sheet. Let set about 15 minutes until the coating looks damp. Deep fry at 375° or until golden brown. Drain well.

Bill Honeycutt
Henrietta, TX

CATFISH BATTER

	catfish	1	egg
1½	cups flour	1	T. mustard
1	cup milk	½	tsp. paprika

SHORE LUNCH
EASY MEAL

Combine batter ingredients until smooth. Dip the catfish in the batter and deep fry.

Dennis Sims
Killen, TX

LAYERED CATFISH DIP

1 lb. catfish fillets or nuggets, cooked	¼ cup red bell pepper, chopped
1 12-oz. pkg. cream cheese, softened	¼ cup yellow bell pepper, chopped
2 T. mayonnaise	pinch garlic salt
2 T. Worcestershire sauce	1 small yellow or white onion, chopped
1 T. lemon juice	1 bottle chili sauce
¼ cup green onions, chopped	fresh parsley, chopped

In a bowl, stir together cream cheese, mayonnaise, Worcestershire sauce, lemon juice, green onion, red and yellow pepper, garlic salt and onion. Spread over the bottom of a plate or serving dish. Then spread the chili sauce over cheese layer. Top with catfish. Sprinkle a little parsley on top and garnish the edge of the plate with parsley and serve with the cracker of your choice.

Will Laxton
St. Louis, MO

CATFISH FRY

8–12 catfish fillets	½ medium onion, grated
24 oz. vegetable or peanut oil	1–2 eggs
1 pt. buttermilk corn bread mix	salt and pepper

In a large skillet, heat oil to 375°. Season fish to taste. Put fish in buttermilk, then in corn bread mix with onions. Place fish in the hot oil. When the fish becomes brown on one side, turn until the other side becomes golden brown.

Bob Rhoads
Mount Vernon, IN

30-MINUTE SOUTHERN-STYLE FISH FRY

1 lb. catfish fillets	⅓ cup yellow corn meal
1 egg	¼ tsp. dried thyme
¼ cup butter or margarine, melted	¼ tsp. salt
	¼ tsp. pepper
1 T. lemon juice	lemon wedges and
½ cup plain bread crumbs	parsley for garnish

Preheat oven to 500°. Spray a 15x10-inch baking pan with nonstick spray and set aside. In a medium bowl beat the egg. In another bowl, stir together butter and lemon juice. On wax paper, combine bread crumbs and the next 4 ingredients. Dip the fillets in the egg, then in corn meal mixture, butter mixture, and the corn meal mixture again. Place in a greased pan and bake until the fillets are golden brown and flake easily with a fork, about 6 minutes per half-inch of thickness. Garnish with lemon and parsley. Serves 4.

Darlene Straman
Stigo, IL

Darlene Straman

DAVE'S BLUE CAT NUGGETS

	catfish fillets	I	tsp. salt	
2	cups white corn meal	½	tsp. pepper	
½	cup flour	4	T. Old Bay Seasoning	

SHORE LUNCH
EASY MEAL

Cut the catfish fillets into small, nugget-size pieces. Then mix all of the above ingredients in a large plastic zip-top bag. Add the catfish and coat thoroughly. Deep fry until they become golden brown.

David Jackson
Chesapeake, VA

David Jackson

FREDDY D'S CATCH AND COOK

2	catfish fillets	½	cup oil for frying
2	eggs	½	cup sharp cheese,
1	cup bread crumbs		grated
1	cup flour		salt and pepper

Put the two eggs, bread crumbs and flour in separate bowls. In an 8-inch frypan, heat the oil. Dip the fillets in the flour first, then egg, and finally in the bread crumbs; then place them in the frypan to cook until done. Place the cooked fillets on a plate, sprinkle with grated cheese. To top it off, scramble the eggs that are left from the batter and place them on top of cheese and fillets. Salt and pepper to taste and enjoy.

Carma Marquez
Sarasota, FL

MORE THAN CATFISH STEW

1	lb. catfish	4	slices fatback
2	cups potatoes, diced	2	qts. water
1	cup onion, chopped		salt (optional)
1	cup carrots, chopped		all purpose Greek
1	cup celery, chopped		seasoning (optional)
4	T. margarine		

Boil the fish and debone it. Put fish into a large pot and add water and onions. Cook for 5 minutes on high. Reduce the heat to medium. In a separate pan, fry out fatback. Add grease and fatback to the fish and onions. Cook for 2 more minutes, add all other ingredients and cook until done. Add water as needed. Serve hot in bowl with corn bread or crackers and a glass of tea. Serves 4.

James Duncan
Aiken, SC

TONY'S SOUTHWESTERN PANFISH

1 lb. fish fillets	1/2 tsp. Old Bay seasoning
2 cups saltine crackers, finely crushed	2 large eggs
1/2 tsp. cayenne pepper	1 cup beer
1/2 tsp. onion powder	4 drops hot pepper sauce
1/2 tsp. garlic powder	oil
1/2 tsp. white pepper	

SHORE LUNCH

EASY MEAL

Mix first six ingredients(excpet the fish) in bowl and set aside. Mix next three ingredients in large bowl and add fish fillets to mixture. Allow to soak for five minutes. Heat oil to 375° for deep frying (oil is ready when a small piece of bread dropped into the oil sinks then rises to the top and begins bubbling away). Take fish fillets one at a time from bowl, allowing excess batter to drip off. Dredge battered fillets through cracker crumb mixture. Place fillets in the oil and fry a few at a time until they are golden brown. Transfer cooked fillets to paper towels to drain excess grease.

Tony Blizzard

Serve with tartar sauce or slices of lemon.

Tony Blizzard
Scottsdale, AZ

BEER BATTERED PANFISH

panfish	I cup corn meal
I can beer	I tsp. onion powder
2 eggs	I tsp. baking powder
I cup flour	I tsp. salt

Mix dry ingredients together, add beer and mix well. Add eggs and beat until batter is smooth (in higher elevations add ¼ cup milk for smoother batter). Dip panfish in batter, brown in oil and bake at 350° for about 30 minutes.

Gilbert Helsley
Hollidaysburg, PA

EASY GRILLED PANFISH FILLETS

panfish fillets	garlic powder
lemon juice	salt and pepper
butter	

Coat fish grid on grill generously with nonstick spray. Place fillets on hot grid over low heat. Baste with melted butter. Sprinkle with lemon juice and garlic powder. Salt and pepper to taste. Grill just until fillets begin to flake. Turn fillets over carefully with spatula. Repeat process with butter, lemon juice, garlic powder, salt and pepper. Grill until fillets flake easily and begin to turn golden brown. Cooking time depends on the thickness of the fillets. Wrap in aluminum foil until ready to serve. Serve with shrimp or seafood sauce.

Connie Griffith
Newton, IL

PAN-FRIED PERCH

4	perch fillets	1	T. fresh basil, chopped
2	cloves garlic, chopped	1	T. turmeric
2	T. butter		fresh lemon juice
2	T. fresh chives, chopped		

Fry garlic in butter. Roll fresh fillets in turmeric, basil and chives. Place fillets and spices in garlic and butter, squeeze lemon juice over fillets. Fry for 10 minutes. Enjoy.

Greg Mchugh
Waverley, NS, Canada

Greg Mchugh

67

PERCH GERMAN POTATO PANCAKES

1 lb. perch fillets	2 cups raw potatoes,
3 eggs, beaten	finely grated
2 T. flour	nutmeg, dash
2 T. onion, grated	pepper, dash
1 T. parsley, chopped	applesauce
2 tsp. salt	

SHORE LUNCH

EASY MEAL

Skin fillets and finely chop. Combine all ingredients except applesauce. Mix thoroughly. Place a well-greased griddle or frypan about 4 inches from hot coals and heat until grease is hot, but not smoking. Drop ⅓ cup fish mixture on griddle and flatten slightly with spatula. Fry 3 to 4 minutes or until brown. Turn carefully and fry 3 to 4 minutes longer or until brown. Drain on paper towel. Keep warm. Serve with applesauce. Serves 6

Glen Anglese
Chicago, IL

STUFFED PERCH FILLETS

8 perch fillets	½ cup bread crumbs
¼ cup butter, melted	3 whole beaten eggs
2 lbs. crab meat (canned	2 T. oil
works best)	dry bread crumbs

Preheat the oven to 375°. Mix melted butter and crab meat together. Stir in ½ cup bread crumbs, mixing well with crab and butter. Place 4 fillets on wax paper and evenly spread the crab mixture over them. Place remaining 4 fillets on top of the mixture to create a "sandwich" look. Coat sandwiched fillets with beaten egg then cover both sides with bread crumbs. Coat a cookie sheet with oil, place the fillets on the cookie sheet and bake for 10 minutes. If you like cheese, place a slice of swiss on the fillets the last 5 minutes of baking time.

Cindy L. Bell
Fort Benning, GA

HERB-ROASTED SALMON

1¼ lbs. salmon fillets with skin intact, cut into six equal pieces	6 T. unsalted butter
3 T. safflower or peanut oil	2 cups mixed fresh herb sprigs (such as chervil, dill, fennel and parsley)

Preheat oven to 400°. Quickly rinse the salmon under cold running water and pat dry with paper towel. Season the salmon to taste with salt and pepper.

Heat oil in a large, heavy oven-proof skillet over high heat. Add 2 or 3 of the fillets, skin-side up, and sauté until lightly browned, about one minute. Turn and sauté the skin side for about 1 minute. Using a wide spatula, remove the fish to a cutting board. With a sharp knife, cut the skin away from each fillet but leave it attached at one end. Top the skin side of each fillet with butter and distribute about half of the herb sprigs over the fillets. Re-position the skin so that it covers the herbs, and return the fillets to the skillet or place in a baking dish. Bake until just done and opaque throughout, about 6 to 8 minutes. Remove the fillets from the oven and discard skin and herbs. To serve, spoon about 2 table-spoons of your favorite white sauce onto each of six dinner plates and place a fillet on top. Garnish with the remaining herb sprigs and serve immediately.

Leo G.J. Seffelaar
Broadview, Saskatchewan, Canada

PACIFIC SALMON TERIYAKI

4	salmon steaks	¼	cup water
½	cup brown sugar	2	T. fresh lemon juice
¼	cup soy sauce		lemon slices

Heat brown sugar, soy sauce, water and lemon juice in a frypan large enough to hold the salmon steaks snugly. Boil, uncovered, stirring occasionally, until the sugar is melted. Add salmon steaks, reduce heat and cover. Simmer salmon steaks for 5 to 6 minutes per side. Remove the steaks and keep warm. Boil the sauce until thickened, about 4 minutes. Serve the salmon steaks drizzled with sauce and garnish with lemon slices.

To barbecue: Prepare sauce as directed above. Marinate steaks in sauce for 10 minutes. Cook on a well-oiled barbecue over medium-high heat for about 4 to 5 minutes per side.

Leo G.J. Seffelaar
Broadview, Saskatchewan, Canada

N.W. SALMON PECAN

4	salmon fillets	1½	T. honey	
⅛	tsp. salt	¼	cup bread crumbs	
⅛	tsp. black pepper	¼	cup pecans, finely	
2	T. Dijon mustard		chopped	
2	T. melted butter	2	tsp. parsley	

Combine Dijon mustard, melted butter and honey. In a separate bowl, combine bread crumbs, chopped pecans and parsley. Sprinkle the salmon with salt and pepper. Place the salmon skin-side down in a greased 13x9-inch pan. Brush mustard mixture on the fillets and spoon the bread crumb mixture over them. Bake at 450° for 15 minutes or until golden brown.

N.W. Lubbers
Louisville, KY

PAN-FRIED SMOKED SALMON WITH HORSERADISH CREAM

12　1-oz. slices smoked salmon	8　sprigs fresh chervil or parsley
freshly ground black pepper	4　T. tomatoes, diced
1　T. olive oil	minced herbs (chives, parsley and dill) for garnish
2　T. whipping cream, whipped	
2　T. prepared horseradish or grated fresh horseradish	

Trim each slice of smoked salmon to 3 to 4 inches in length and 1 to 2 inches in width. Season to taste with pepper. Place a large skillet over high heat, film the pan with the olive oil and fry the salmon slices for 10 to 15 seconds on one side only. Arrange 3 salmon slices, fried side up, on each of 4 plates. In a small bowl, combine the whipped cream and horseradish. Spoon or pipe the horseradish cream onto the plates. Place 2 chervil or parsley sprigs and 1 tablespoon tomatoes on each plate and sprinkle with some of the minced herbs.

Dwight K. Schwappe
Saint Helens, OR

GRILLED TROUT

1	trout	1	sliced onion	
1/8	tsp. salt	1/8	tsp. garlic salt	
1/8	tsp. black pepper	1/8	tsp. paprika	
1	lemon wedge	1	T. butter	

Clean fish out and remove the head. Wash in lukewarm water. Peel skin back to the base of the tail. Add ingredients to all sides and middle of trout. Place skin over meat. Double wrap in aluminum foil. Place on grill for 15 minutes on each side. Remove foil and skin. Enjoy!!

Eric Peoples
Carthage, MO

BAKED HONEY APPLE TROUT

1	trout	1	slice bacon	
1	T. butter	1	lemon wedge	
1/2	tsp. honey		salt and pepper	
1/2	tsp. applesauce		lemon juice	

Lay out a piece of aluminum foil 6 inches longer than trout. Divide butter, honey and applesauce and apply to foil in 2 equal lengths. Both lengths should be on top and bottom of the lateral line of the fish. Put one slice of bacon inside the trout. Salt and pepper to taste. Wrap and bake in preheated oven at 350° for 35 minutes. Sprinkle with lemon juice at serving.

Gerald Davis
Milanville, PA

SPICY TROUT FILLETS

4 rainbow trout, skinned and filleted	salt and pepper
2 T. cooking oil	Cajun seasoning

SHORE LUNCH
EASY MEAL

Heat oil in frying pan to medium high. Place fillets in hot oil and sprinkle with salt, pepper and Cajun seasoning. When first side is slightly brown, turn and sprinkle other side with seasonings. Fillets are done when the fish flakes when stuck with a fork. Serves 4.

Elmer Stoneman
Mocksville, NC

Elmer Stoneman

FISH RECIPE

6	fish fillets	2	T. flour
2	eggs		bread crumbs
I	cup milk		oil
I	T. steak seasoning		

Soak fish fillets in salt water for 2 hours. Drain fish, dry with paper towel and put aside. Mix eggs, milk, steak seasoning and flour until smooth. Put bread crumbs in another bowl. Dip the fish first in the egg mixture and then in the bread crumbs. Fry them in oil (not deep fry) for 5 minutes on each side or until lightly browned. Put the fillets in a covered dish and cook them in the microwave for 2 minutes on high and then let them stand for 10 minutes. Each recipe can be increased or decreased depending on how much fish you have.

Hermann Heeschen
Ontario, Canada

Hermann Heeschen

EASY FISH FAVORITES

1 medium fillet	carrots, sliced
⅛ tsp. salt	onions, chopped
⅛ tsp. pepper	green peppers, sliced
½ tsp. dried basil	1 T. butter
potatoes, thinly sliced	

Place cleaned fillet on an 18- to 20-inch piece of foil (bigger if you catch a lunker). Sprinkle with salt, pepper and dried basil. Put a few thin potato slices, carrots, onions, green peppers and a tablesoon of butter on foil with fillet. Sprinkle a little more salt and pepper on the veggies and then wrap up the package and seal the ends. Put the package on the grill, grate or right on the coals, if you like. In 15 or 20 minutes open the package and check the contents with a fork. The fish should flake and the veggies should be soft. If not, wrap it back up and cook it longer.

Christopher T. Black
Tualatin, OR

Christopher T. Black

FAVORITE RECIPE

1 lb. fillets	1/4 cup white wine
1 bay leaf	1/4 cup water
5 peppercorns	1 T. pickle relish
1/2 rib celery, cut into 1/2-inch pieces	salt and pepper
1/2 medium carrot, cut into 1/2-inch pieces	

Combine water, wine, bay leaf and peppercorns and bring to a simmer. Add the fish and cook until opaque. It will have a nice white look and can be easily flaked. Remove the fish and let it cool. After the fish has cooled, flake it and mix it with chopped celery, chopped carrot, mayonnaise and 1 spoon of pickle relish. This can be used for sandwiches or as a cocktail spread on crackers.

Arthur Dolgan
Delray Beach, FL

BREADED FISH FILLETS

2 fillets	1 can regular beer (can be flat)
8 peppercorns	salt and pepper
1 whole lemon, sliced and seeded	
4–6 T. margarine or butter, melted	

SHORE LUNCH

EASY MEAL

Place seasoned fillets skin-side down in a metal or glass baking pan. Pour beer around fillets in pan. Pour melted margarine or butter on each fillet and scatter peppercorns evenly in the pan. Bake at 350° for 30 to 40 minutes or until fish is golden brown and flakes easily. Garnish with lemon slices.

Jean Jensen
Lufkin, TX

OVEN FRIED FISH

2 lbs. skinless fillets	¼ tsp. pepper
I cup instant mashed	2 eggs, beaten
potato flakes	¼ cup melted margarine
I pkg. garlic/Italian salad	or butter
dressing mix	paprika

Combine potato flakes, salad dressing mix and pepper in a shallow dish. Dip fish into egg and roll in potato mixture. Place the fish in a single layer on a well-greased bake-and-serve platter, 16x10 inches. Pour margarine over fish. Pour beaten egg remains over and sprinkle with paprika. Preheat oven to 500° and bake for 13 to 15 miutes or until the fish flakes easily. Be sure to cover the platter while cooking.

John W. Borrini
Orangeburg, SC

CANNED FISH

any kind of fish	I T. ketchup
I T. oil	I T. salt
I T. vinegar	

Clean and cut up fish and pack in pint jars. Add remaining ingredients to each jar. Cook for 4 hours in a canner or at 10 lbs. pressure for 90 minutes. Suckers or red horse work best for this recipe.

Norma Blank
Shawano, WI

FISH IN A HUSK

6 medium-size fillets	hot sauce
6 ears corn on the cob	garlic salt
1 cup butter, melted	

Carefully remove the husks from the ears of corn. Set the corn cobs aside. Place the husks in tub of water and soak for ½ hour. Place soaked husks on the table and arrange each to form a pocket. Place each fillet into a husk. Pour a portion of hot butter over fillet, then add several shakes hot sauce. Add garlic salt to your taste. Close the husk around the fillet and tie with string. Do the same with remaining fillets and husks. Place on hot grill or steamer for 15-20 minutes. Spray the husks with water occasionally to keep them from drying out or burning. For smoking, do not close the husk around the fillets. Smoke for 1 hour.

Use the corn on the cob as a side dish. Butter and wrap the corn in foil, then grill along side the fillets for 45 minutes. Start the corn first for better timing. Serve the fillets right in the husk.

Stanley Ortoski
Sheffield Lake, OH

LEMON PEPPER STRIPS

3 cups yellow corn meal	4 tsp. lemon pepper	
1 cup flour	3 eggs	
1 tsp. salt	1 cup milk	

Mix corn meal, flour, salt and lemon pepper. Combine the eggs and milk. Dip the fillet strips in the egg and milk, then roll in the corn meal mixture, coating completely. Fry in oil until golden brown.

Bill Bowman
Louisville, KY

FISH STEAKS WITH HERBS

	fish steaks	¼	tsp. thyme
6	T. butter	1	tsp. salt
1	clove garlic, chopped	2	T. lemon juice
⅓	cup onion, chopped	¾	cup fresh bread
¼	tsp. tarragon		crumbs
1	T. parsley		

Arrange steaks in baking dish. Sauté butter and garlic until tender. Remove garlic. Add onions and sauté a few minutes. Stir in remaining ingredients except bread crumbs. Spoon about ½ of the mixture over the fish. Add crumbs to remaining mixture and spread on top of the fish. Bake in preheated oven at 400° for 25 minutes.

Bob Dotson
East Peoria, IL

FISH FRY TO PERFECTION

	fish, chunked	2	green onions, diced	
1	bottle hot sauce	1	red onion, diced	
2	cucumbers, diced	2–3	limes	
3	tomatoes, diced	1	lemon	
1	onion, diced			

Chop the fish into small chunks and put into a large bowl. Finely dice the vegetables. Next squeeze the limes and lemon into a bowl with the vegetables and fish; add a little salt and stir all around. Mix in bottle of hot sauce and heat oil in skillet. Fry until fish flakes and vegetables soften.

Rick Holguin
Upland, CA

SHRIMP STUFFING

¼ cup shrimp, deveined	¼ cup green onion,
½ cup grated Havarti or	sliced with tops
Swiss cheese	½ tsp. dill
½ tsp. salt	2 T. mayonnaise

Mix the shrimp, cheese, onions, salt, dill and mayonnaise together. Use to stuff fillets of dressed fish. Yields stuffing for 1½ lbs. of fish.

Leo G.J. Seffelaar
Broadview, Saskatchewan, Canada

BASIC TARTAR SAUCE

½ cup mayonnaise or	2 T. fresh lime or lemon
salad dressing	juice
2 T. sweet pickle relish,	2 tsp. onion, finely
chopped	chopped
2 T. sour cream	⅛ tsp. salt

In a small bowl, mix all ingredients. Chill at least 30 minutes to blend flavors. Recipe can be doubled.

Susan Burroughs
Paragould, AR

CORN MEAL COATING FOR CATFISH

½ cup corn meal	1 tsp. chili powder
2 tsp. seasoned salt	

Mix ingredients. Dip slightly damp or wet pieces of fish in the corn meal mix and fry in your favorite shortening or oil.

Norman Bauer
Warrensburg, MO

RUB FOR BAKING FRESH FISH

¼ cup sea salt	1 pinch each cayenne
½ tsp. ground black	pepper, parsley,
pepper	oregano
¼ tsp. basil	olive oil

Mix dry ingredients and combine any additional spices you enjoy. Lightly coat fish in olive oil and sprinkle salt-based mixture on the fish and bake. If you rub the mixture directly on the fish, avoid the olive oil, cut back the sea salt and increase the other ingredients. Works on any species of fish.

Ferrill Standage
Victoria, KS